WEST'S LAW SCHOOL
ADVISORY BOARD

BIOETHICS
AND LAW
IN A NUTSHELL

By

SANDRA H. JOHNSON

Professor Emerita of Law and Health Care Ethics
Saint Louis University School of Law

ROBERT L. SCHWARTZ

Henry Weihofen Professor of Law
and Professor of Pediatrics
University of New Mexico School of Law

11/10

WEST®

A Thomson Reuters business

Mat #11591493

© 2009 Thomson Reuters

610 Opperman Drive
St. Paul, MN 55123
1–800–313–9378

Printed in the United States of America

ISBN: 978–0–314–06668–8

*To the memory of those of our parents
who have completed their life journeys,
Mary and Clarence ("Tacky") Hanneken
and Jerome Schwartz*

S.H.J. and R.L.S.

*

PREFACE

For more than twenty years, we have been co-authors, with Barry Furrow, Tim Greaney, and Tim Jost, of Health Law: Cases, Materials and Problems, which is now in its Sixth Edition. The Health Law casebook has always included substantial coverage of bioethics issues, and the bioethics chapters have also been published, with additional material, as Bioethics: Health Care Law and Ethics. As those familiar with the casebooks will recognize, a few parts of this Nutshell are taken directly from one or the other of those casebooks. This Nutshell grows out of our experiences in writing these casebooks and in teaching our students over the years.

Our aim in this Nutshell is to provide students with a brief and accessible introductory overview of the central legal issues in bioethics. This volume is not meant to be, and is not, comprehensive. Our readers certainly will be able to list issues that we have not included.

Our concern is to provide a foundation for legal analysis of the most durable bioethics issues that have consistently found themselves at the center of the public debate over the last quarter of a century, not to address all of the issues that have made an appearance in that debate. Our focus is on the legal issues, and these materials primarily address issues that have found their way into the courts, legislatures, and administrative agencies in the United States. We have included only a brief chapter to provide a precis of the more influential ethical theories at play in bioethics discussions. This Nutshell provides the overview—the forest, if you will; you will have to go elsewhere to study the individual trees in more detail.

We have enjoyed writing this book, but mostly we have enjoyed collaborating for more than two decades now. One of the things we enjoy is that we do not agree with each other on several quite significant issues, and you may even notice this tension in the text. We have tried to be evenhanded, and we hope that we have explained how reasonable people can hold very different views on the propriety of applying law to almost every issue in bioethics.

As always, we are grateful to the students who assisted us in the preparation of this text: Cara Jackson and Kathryn Krieger of Saint Louis University School of Law and Katey Cortese of University of California, Hastings College of the Law. We are grateful as well to the decades of students who have made us think and express ourselves more clearly. We also thank our deans, Jeffrey Lewis and

Kevin Washburn for their continuing support. Finally, we thank our families, far and wide, for their constant love.

SANDRA H. JOHNSON
ROBERT L. SCHWARTZ

September 2009

*

OUTLINE

OUTLINE

TABLE OF CASES

References are to Pages

TABLE OF CASES

BIOETHICS
AND LAW
IN A NUTSHELL

*

CHAPTER 1

INTRODUCTION TO ETHICS

I. ETHICAL THEORIES

Most general theories of ethics can be categorized as either consequentialist or deontological. Consequentialist theories, like utilitarianism, judge the moral or ethical quality of an act solely by the end it achieves, the consequences that follow from it. Deontological theories are those that examine the morality of an act on grounds other than the results it produces. In deontological theories, moral content is independent of consequences.

Most people, including bioethicists and judges, draw from both of these categories in deciding what ought to be done. Arguments centered on the consequences of a particular action or rule—e.g., that scientific research will or will not flourish—often stand opposed to arguments that essential human characteristics demand certain restrictions—e.g., that human dignity demands that individuals cannot be used as experimental subjects without their consent. Often, however, consequential analysis and deontological analysis arrive at the same place, although for different reasons. For example, one may see it argued that respecting individual rights to consent voluntarily to participating as a human subject increases support for the research enterprise itself and contributes to its thriving.

A. Utilitarianism

Utilitarianism is the most familiar of the consequentialist theories, and has exerted significant influence in arguments about bioethics issues. Utilitarianism argues that the justification of acts lies only in their consequences, and that the desired consequences are those that maximize utility, measured as the aggregated happiness of the whole society.

Utilitarianism takes two major forms. "Act utilitarianism" focuses on the consequences of each individual act. "Rule utilitarianism" focuses on the consequences of rules that guide conduct. It adds to act utilitarianism the impact of the decisions of individual actors across society. Rule utilitarianism is especially compatible with legal decision making as it will reject the individual act, which as a single act maximizes utility, if that same act, if followed generally or made a rule of behavior, would have a negative outcome on aggregate happiness.

A key challenge in utilitarianism is the identification and measurement of utility, happiness, or benefit. Persons may disagree with what constitutes happiness or benefit and how it is to be measured. One individual's pain or burden must be compared to another's happiness to decide whether the act under consideration produces aggregate gain or loss. This challenge is magnified in the evaluation of the distribution of benefits and burdens (utility and disutility) across society as most actions produce uneven or unequal distribution even when the aggregate effect is to increase utility overall.

Utilitarianism does not mark particular actions— such as murder, rape, lying, fraud—as inherently unethical. Rather, the acts are to be measured by their aggregate consequences alone. This does not mean that utilitarianism accepts such acts as moral. Utilitarians instead argue that a consequentialist analysis standing alone will itself reject such actions because of their negative consequences for society as a whole.

B. Deontological Theories

1. Kantianism

Immanuel Kant's work in philosophy is a leading alternative to utilitarianism and is evident in much of the analysis of modern bioethics. Kantianism rejects consequentialism and measures the morality of an action primarily by whether it arises from a "good will." This sense of good will is not the equivalent of having a good heart or good intention. Rather, good will for Kant refers to the individual's character or moral goodness. One who acts in a morally acceptable way only because it produces benefits for himself rather than out of a sense of moral duty is acting in a way that does not have intrinsic moral worth. True moral worth is evidenced by actions based on duty rather than personal inclination or consequences.

Kantianism categorizes duties as either perfect or imperfect. Perfect duties produce rights on the part of others—they may demand performance. Imperfect duties do not support claims of right. The duty to refrain from unjustly harming another is an example of a perfect duty, while the related duty to contribute to the well-being of others is an imperfect duty. Perfect duties take precedence over imperfect duties when they conflict. As with all theories, Kantianism faces challenges and disputes in identifying the content and application of these duties in specific circumstances.

For Kant, moral principles are universal rather than subjective or relative. His unconditional "Categorical Imperative" states: "I ought to never act except in such a way that I could also will my maxim should become universal law." Kant argues that the Categorical Imperative does not focus on the consequences of the act, but rather on universal principles of morality and the good character of the actor.

In Kant's view, rational individuals acting in freedom will reason to shared moral values. Kant's philosophy asserts a strong priority for autonomy by focusing on the choices of the individual even while it assumes that the individual is bound by freely discerned and freely accepted moral principles. In addition, the moral equality of all persons is essential to Kantianism. This requires that all individuals be treated as moral beings and prohibits using persons as instruments, as means to an end.

These principles of autonomy and moral equality have exerted substantial influence in bioethics.

2. Natural Law

Traditional natural law theories of ethics rely both on the acceptance of a God who guides human beings through divine providence and on the inherent character of human beings as rational actors who know and can choose, or not, to act in accord with this divine guidance. Under natural law theory, human beings are naturally drawn to morally proper actions.

As a religiously-grounded theory, natural law may be rejected as inappropriate justification for public policy and legal standards. Some modern forms of natural law theory, however, argue in favor of a secular version of the theory. They rely on humanism, which values human beings as rational and transcendent, with an innate understanding of right principles and values.

Natural law theory maintains that the good has inherent value, apart from any of its consequences or effects. Life, knowledge, procreation, and friendship, for example, are aspects of the good under natural law theory, without any calculation of benefits to the individual or group.

Natural law theory holds that some acts are intrinsically and absolutely evil and can never be performed ethically. The natural law principle of "double effect," however, provides a tool for guiding action when a moral act produces both good and evil effects. Under double effect, the act in question must itself be morally good or at least neutral; the actor must have an intent to do the good and would avoid the bad effect if possible; the good effect must be produced by the action and not by the bad effect itself; and the good done must outweigh the bad effect.

This principle has been used in bioethics in a variety of situations, but most prominently in evaluating aggressive pain management where there has been a concern that the necessary medications may hasten the patient's dying. The application of double effect in this circumstance was recognized as a legal principle in Justice Rehnquist's opinion for the majority in Vacco v. Quill, 521 U.S. 793, 117 S.Ct. 2293, 138 L.Ed.2d 834 (1997). See Section II in Chapter 6.

II. APPLIED ETHICS

Both consequentialism and deontology are apparent in applied form in the various approaches to bioethics. These approaches have influenced health care practice, public policy, and law.

A. Principlism

Principlism has been the most influential approach in bioethics. Courts have frequently adopted principlism explicitly in decisions regarding care at the end of life.

Principlism relies on "midlevel principles," i.e., it applies principles that are believed to be generally held rather than developing a general theory to justify these principles or individual acts. The core principles in this approach are truth-telling, autonomy, non-maleficence, beneficence, and distributive justice. These principles can be derived from, or justified by, both consequentialism and deontological theories.

These principles provide a guide for examining particular issues. So, for example, the principle of truth-telling argues that the doctor should reveal a terminal diagnosis to the patient; and autonomy argues in favor of allowing the competent patient to make the ultimate decision concerning his course of treatment. Non-maleficence captures the traditional medical principle of "do no harm," and beneficence requires that the health care professional or other decision maker act in the best interests of the patient.

Principlism, like any general or applied ethical theory, confronts some challenges. First, the demands of the principles may conflict. For example, a competent individual's decision may appear to be harmful to himself, and thus, autonomy and beneficence may appear to conflict. For example, a competent person who refuses effective, recommended treatment may be viewed as acting against his or her own best interests.

Principlism first requires that apparent conflicts among principles be closely examined to assure that a false conflict is not being asserted. For generations, for example, physicians argued that disclosure of a terminal diagnosis was always inconsistent with their duty to do no harm, and this may be viewed as a false conflict in all but rare circumstances. Similarly, when social notions of a patient's best interests conflict with the patient's choice, this may simply represent a disagreement over the assessment of the interests of the patient rather than a conflict between autonomy and beneficence. In general, however, where conflicts do occur, principlism tends to give primacy to autonomy or personal choice in most, although not all, circumstances.

A second challenge to principlism is the criticism that the analysis tends to focus too narrowly on the interests of the patient alone, to the exclusion of the interests of the family or the health care professional or broader social concerns. Critics also argue that principlism in practice tends to neglect the social and economic context and consequences of health care decisions even though the approach recognizes distributive justice as a relevant principle.

B.   Feminist Bioethics

Feminist bioethics offers an alternative to principlism in several respects. The many variations on feminism that fall within the umbrella of feminist bioethics share a commitment to the importance of understanding the social and economic context for the health care decision at issue. For example, some morally significant choices for patients may be severely constrained by inadequate financial and social support for the elderly, ill, or disabled and their caregivers. Feminist bioethics also widens the relevant circle of concern beyond the patient to include the well-being of family members. Feminist bioethics theories tend to share a primary concern for health care issues affecting women, whether as patients or as caregivers who most often will bear a direct burden in realizing the patient's choices.

Feminist bioethics encompasses the several forms of feminist philosophy, and these may conflict in the analysis of particular bioethics issues. Liberal feminism focuses on the equality of men and women and argues that women are entitled to equal rights and equal opportunity. Liberal feminism distrusts the allocation of rights, responsibilities, and opportunities along gender lines, even when apparently to the benefit of women, because female stereotypes have unjustly limited women under the guise of offering protection. Cultural or relational feminism highlights gender differences and argues that apparently neutral rules that treat men and women the same can treat women unfairly. This form of feminist theory argues that male paradigms dominate apparently neutral value systems, including the principlist approach, and ignore female value systems that rely on an ethic of caring or a more relational approach to decision making. Radical feminism also relies on gender differences, but argues that these are produced by the oppression of women, and that legal standards ought to protect women more actively from male oppression. Finally, post-modern approaches to feminism reject generalizations and analyze each individual situation.

C. Critical Race Theory and Bioethics

Critical race theory argues that legal and ethical decisions cannot be analyzed apart from the political, social, and economic systems within which they arise, and particularly as these relate to issues of race. Critical race theory argues, for example, that the application of apparently neutral principles reflects the dominant culture and denies values that emerge from a more racially and culturally diverse experience. Reliance on individual autonomy and choice, for example, can operate to the detriment of persons of color in systems that are essentially unjust. Social justice and equality are core concerns that are arguably neglected in other approaches.

At a minimum, critical race theory argues that the perspective of race is essential, including the perspective that is informed by the cultural history of medical care in the U.S. This history reveals oppression of minorities in several respects. Forcible or deceptive use of African–Americans as subjects in medical experiments, for example, produced medical advances ultimately denied to minority populations due to discrimination in health care services and exclusion from professional medical education. See Section I in Chapter 8.

D. Religious Perspectives in Bioethics

Religious perspectives on issues in bioethics vary considerably, as would be expected with the diversity of religious viewpoints in the U.S. Scholarship from a religious perspective contributes to the body of work in bioethics, and religious leaders participate in public policy debates on bioethics, some more vigorously than others. In addition, legal standards sometimes, although not always, accommodate religious perspectives of individuals in health care decision making. See, e.g., Section IV.B below; Section II.C in Chapter 4; Section VI in Chapter 5; and Section IV.C in Chapter 3.

Some religious perspectives have had a significant influence on the legal framework of particular bioethics issues. In particular, Catholic perspectives on end-of-life care provided the framework used for end-of-life decision making when that issue first reached the courts. Early judicial decisions relied on papal statements concerning the permissibility of withdrawing ventilator support and the primacy of the patient's will. In addition, concepts such as the principle of double effect continue to have influence in law. See Section I.B.2, above.

There are, however, areas of considerable conflict as well between principles that arise from particular religious beliefs and views held by most citizens. This appears to be the case, for example, in regard to legal rights to abortion, physician-assisted suicide or physician aid in dying, and in standards concerning the withdrawal of life-sustaining nutrition and hydration in a narrow band of situations. In such cases, religious advocates argue that their perspective has a place in the public debate and that it offers principles that will preserve or create a better society. When religious perspectives take on the force of law or have other power to impose themselves on individuals who do not share those beliefs, however, many argue that religious approaches to bioethics overstep appropriate boundaries and violate the tolerance that marks civil, secular society.

E. Virtue Ethics

Virtue ethics argues, like Kantian ethics, that the character of the individual actor is a core concern in evaluating the propriety of particular actions. In addition, personal virtues, including honesty and competency for example, lead to right action. Virtue ethics is particularly influential in traditional medical ethics, which focuses on the essential character of medicine and what the good doctor should be and do.

Virtue ethics values the moral agency of health care professionals and argues that other approaches to bioethics mistakenly make professionals the instruments of the patients alone. In turn, critics argue that virtue ethics supports the hegemony of the medical profession. Legal protection of health care professionals' rights to refuse to participate in particular forms of treatment is consistent with virtue ethics but is quite controversial for its effect on patients. See Section IV.B, below.

F.   Methodological Approaches

1.   Casuistry

Casuistry is a methodological approach that is quite familiar to law students. Casuistry seeks to discover the proper course of action through a case-based approach, requiring a close examination of the facts in each circumstance and asking whether the current case is more like or unlike other cases previously considered. Rather than deriving general principles from theory, casuistry develops principles from case analysis. Marshaling an accurate and adequately rich accounting of the facts of a case is a challenge in casuistry just as it is in law.

2.   Pragmatism

Pragmatism begins with an acceptance of the diversity of viewpoints and values that informs health care decisions. It argues that practical knowledge of how systems work and respect for divergent views will produce the proper rule or action.

3.   Narrative Bioethics

Narrative bioethics relies on a methodology of storytelling. This approach affirms the value of different experiences of the same event. It argues that clarification of proper action can emerge from the stories told by individuals themselves—patients, physicians, nurses, family members, and others.

III. DISTRIBUTIVE JUSTICE

The field of bioethics thus far has focused primarily on medical treatment decisions, creating what is essentially an ethics of the bedside, even though principlism has long recognized the principle of distributive justice. Issues arising in health care reform and more specific issues concerning allocation of scarce or restricted health care resources are gaining increased attention and spotlighting norms for the distribution of scarce or shared resources.

The general theories of ethics discussed above may be employed in these questions. A utilitarian approach, for example, would assess the distribution of health care services by examining its consequences on society as a whole. A deontological approach may focus on analyzing where the moral duty lies and how respect for the moral equality of persons would be affected by particular distribution systems. Analysis of the moral character of distribution of health care resources typically begins with addressing one issue: whether health care is distinguishable from other goods and services that are governed by market transactions.

Health care may be viewed as unique, or at least special, because the social costs of disease and disability impair the functioning of society generally, or because health is required for human functioning and identity, or because the relief of suffering is a special imperative, or because the unequal original distribution of health and illness creates unfair competition among citizens. Egalitarian and communitarian approaches, for example, argue that society has an obligation to its members to provide basic minimal care, however that may be defined, either because it is the only way to assure equal opportunity or because respect for persons requires it. Utilitarians may argue that the social costs of avoidable disease and illness outweigh the cost of providing basic care, or vice versa.

Others argue that health care is a consumer good like any other, and lack of health care is the result of personal choices and should remain so. Libertarians, for example, may support a market approach to distribution because redistributing wealth is unjust to those from whom it is taken. Law and economics, a form of consequentialism, may argue that the market is the appropriate mechanism for distributing health care. Providing health care as a matter of right, according to this argument, would create disincentives for self-support, inefficiencies because of the added cost of the distribution system, and excessive utilization because of the separation of payment and consumption.

IV. THE RELATIONSHIP
OF LAW AND ETHICS

A. Generally

Law and ethics are not identical. Some believe that the law is too blunt an instrument to deal with the delicate, intimate, and highly variable situations that characterize bioethics. In fact, some view the participation of lawyers in health care decisions, for example through ethics committees or institutional review boards or in hospital policy-making, as counterproductive. Others argue that the law is essential to protect patients from medical dominance and overreaching.

One may assume that all substantial ethical obligations should be supported by the force of law. Paradoxically, however, the "legalization" of an obligation, like the "medicalization" of a personal or social problem, may produce undesired consequences. A specific law intended to deter bad behavior, encourage desired behavior, or protect the vulnerable can instead encourage gaming, avoidance, and defensive action to the detriment of patients. Legal standards setting a floor for accepted behavior are criticized for stimulating a drive to the bottom and a diminution of the commitment to ethical behavior. Law is also limited by the cost or intrusiveness of any enforcement process, the variability of context, and even by the lack of consensus on ethical norms. It is usually understood, then, that obligations defined by law do not encompass the complete moral obligations of the health care professional, or the family, or the patient.

Law and ethics often converge, however. One point of convergence between law and ethics is the explicit adoption of ethical norms and ethical modes of reasoning in regulation and case law. A second point of convergence occurs in shared methodologies between law and ethics, which is most apparent in casuistry. See Section II.F.1, above.

The culture and norms of the legal system contribute particular values in bioethics debates. Law tends to emphasize consistency and equal treatment, for example, as primary principles. Law generally champions individual rights and personal autonomy over relationships. In addition, law contributes a very strong respect for procedure over a particular outcome. Standards adopted in legislation and case law have addressed some thorny issues in bioethics by specifying the procedure that should be used to resolve a conflict rather than by deciding the substantive outcome.

The values in law at times have conflicted with established ethical norms and culture of the health professions. In some circumstances, legal norms may have overtaken medical norms, for example when case law created a duty of informed consent or recognized the authority of the patient and family to make decisions concerning discontinuation of life-sustaining treatment. Even here, however, dialogue among law and medicine and ethics continues. Some argue, in fact, that law ultimately surrendered to medical interests against informed consent and that law did no more than recognize emerging medical standards for end-of-life care.

The reliance of law on the adversarial process has been particularly criticized in bioethics. There is great support for alternative dispute mechanisms and extra-legal processes such as ethics committees, which actually were thrust into prominence by judicial opinions.

B. Conflicts of Conscience and Law

A substantial portion of the law of bioethics governs the scope of individual liberties in regard to health care decision making. Many of the legal boundaries on individual decision making, such as legal limitations on abortion; the prohibition in most states against physician-assisted suicide or physician aid in dying; and participation in medical experimentation, are discussed elsewhere in this text.

Debates over boundaries on individual choice typically contest the appropriate relationship of law and morality. Some argue that the law's power used to restrict care believed necessary or desirable by an individual patient enforces a moral, ethical, or religious perspective illegitimately. Others argue that the law must prohibit individual choice to engage in immoral behavior that damages the social fabric or injures vulnerable persons.

Particular ethical and legal issues arise when an individual patient and the health care professional disagree as to the morality of medical interventions permitted by law. In this context, both parties assert claims to moral agency, personal liberty, and, perhaps, religious freedom. Individual patients claim a right to make their own moral judgment as to whether to receive treatment that is permitted by law; and individual professionals and health care facilities claim a right to refrain from participating in actions they view as immoral even if permitted by law. These conflicts arise in any number of health care treatment decisions, but have most prominently concerned abortion, contraception, physician-assisted suicide or physician aid in dying, and euthanasia and may be re-emerging in regard to medically provided nutrition and hydration.

Some argue that health care professionals and health care organizations surrender some personal liberty when they choose to enter the health care field and should be bound to provide all care allowed by law as needed. If they are not willing to provide that care, they should leave the practice or at least confine their field of work. Others argue that health care professionals are themselves moral beings who may never be forced to compromise their moral principles or subject their own moral agency to the will of another. If the ethics and character of the health professions is compromised, they argue that the power of the professions becomes dangerous. Most public policy responses to these claims of conscience seek to balance the claims of patients and health care professionals.

Legislative response to conscience claims over the past three decades have attempted to balance the need of patients for timely medical care, respect for the moral decisions of both patients and health care professionals. Legal responses also try to accommodate the interests of some health care facilities in abiding by their religious mission and others in providing services to patients when individual employees or staff are refusing to participate. In some situations, these interests are amenable to compromise, for example, where the care is quite easily available elsewhere, although some parties find any compromise unacceptable. In other circumstances, the interests are not easily accommodated, as where care delayed is care denied.

Typically, legislation and regulation extending legal protection (from liability, denial of government funding, or adverse employment actions) to health care professionals refusing to provide legal health care services set boundaries on the right of refusal. These boundaries exist as limitations on the services that may be refused; limitations on the categories of professionals that may fall within the scope of protection; limitations on the bases for objection that are recognized and accorded protection; conditional rather than unconditional protection for refusals depending on the availability of alternative providers; or particular preconditions for the exercise of refusal to participate that may include specific notice to prospective patients, required referrals for services, timely notice to employers, and so on.

Early legislative efforts on both the federal and state levels addressed particular listed services only, focusing primarily on abortion and euthanasia. Typical legislation currently addresses specific interventions. Some legislative "conscience clauses" appear as a provision within broader legislation. It is quite common, for example, for state legislation on advance directives to recognize a right on the part of health care professionals to refuse to comply with the terms of the directive. For discussion of advance directives, see Section IV.B in Chapter 5. Some legislative and regulatory conscience provisions are broader.

Some legislation extends the right of refusal to both religious and moral, non-religious objections. Both categories present challenges in scope. Limiting recognition to religious objections only, for example, triggers issues in deciding what counts as "religious" or a "religion" and whether religious perspectives should be favored over secular moral perspectives. A more expansive scope that recognizes non-religious moral perspectives creates boundary issues regarding the basis for refusal to participate. Disputes over the course of treatment for a particular patient in particular circumstances, for example, may appear as conflicts over the morality of continuing treatment in light of its burdens or as an assertion of professional ethics in regard to patient care.

Health care organizations experience the conscientious objection issue in two forms. First, as employers, these organizations are concerned about the effect of protection of conscience on their ability to deliver care to patients. Although most facilities support some protection, the broader it is, the more difficult the management challenges. Second, health care facilities may themselves claim protection for their refusal to provide certain forms of treatment when to do so would violate their, usually religious, mission.

Extending conscience protections to health care facilities may attract support in response to the contribution made by these facilities, but it may deny needed treatment to patients if there are no other facilities that provide easy and timely access to the care. Some argue as well that allowing facilities to exclude citizens requiring care allowed in law is inconsistent with the provision of extensive public funds through Medicare and Medicaid payments, support for research, support for residency training, and exemption from income and property taxes. Currently, conscience legislation permits health care facilities to refuse to provide particular services under certain narrow circumstances only. This remains a contentious issue.

CHAPTER 2

HUMAN REPRODUCTION

I. DEFINING A HUMAN BEING— ETHICS AND LAW

A. Introduction

The starting point for evaluating the ethical and legal arguments that surround abortion must be the definition of personhood. Yet, our society has had difficulty defining who is a "person." In part, this arises out of the different and inconsistent purposes for which we seek a definition. The "person" from whom we wish to harvest a kidney for transplantation may be defined differently from the "person" who is protected by the Fourteenth Amendment, federal civil rights laws, and various other federal and state laws. Even when the purpose of the definition is settled—as when we seek to know who is a person able to bring an action under state tort law—there is no consensus on when the status of "personhood" first attaches. The most obvious definition of personhood is a recursive one: a human being (a "person") is the reproductive product of other human beings. Even if we accept this "human stock" definition of person, however, the inquiry remains open. That human stock could become a person, for various different legal purposes, upon conception, quickening, viability, birth, or some other time.

Further, the definition of "person" need not be limited to various stages in the development of human stock. Some people would reject the "human stock" definition altogether. "Personhood" could commence upon ensoulment, upon the development of self concept, upon the development of a sense of personal history, or upon the ability to communicate through language, all attributes that arguably could attach to entities that are not the result of human reproduction, like other primates or computer driven machines. The resolution of the question appears to require a resort to first principles.

In the vast majority of cases, it is not difficult to distinguish a person from something else. You are easily distinguishable from your arms, your dog, your insurance company and your gold bust of Elvis, as close as you may feel to each of them. The most difficult questions tend to arise at the very beginning and at the very end of human life. Just as you may be able to identify the fact that you were in love, but not be able to identify exactly when it began, or the moment when it ended, the beginnings and the endings of "personhood" are the fuzzy portions.

There are limits to what may reasonably be considered a "person," even when we limit our consideration to human stock. Few suggest that anything independent of the unified sperm and ovum, or its consequences, ought to be considered a person, although advances in cloning and cellular manipulation may challenge this assumption. A great many religious groups consider "personhood" to attach at conception. Aristotle viewed the development of the person as a three stage process, going from vegetable (at conception), to animal (in utero), to rational (sometime after birth). For many centuries, Christian theology fixed the point of "immediate animation" when the fetus was "ensouled" as forty days after conception for males and eighty days after conception for females. St. Thomas Aquinas determined that the ensoulment took place at the time of quickening, usually fourteen to eighteen weeks after conception, and his determination had a very substantial effect on the development of the common law in England and in this country.

Others who focus on the biological product of human reproduction may see the advent of a new human being at the time of the development of genetically distinct ova, which occurs before the mother's own birth, or perhaps at fertilization, or perhaps at the time of the implantation of the fertilized ovum, which is the medical beginning of a pregnancy. Still others rationally define the moment of "personhood" as the moment there is the first sign of the neural streak, which will later turn into the brain, or perhaps at the time of the first signs of the circulatory system, or perhaps at the time of quickening, or viability. Many, of course, find the magic moment at birth, and in some societies the survival outside the womb for a year (or more) after birth, is the defining "personhood" moment.

Some philosophers have suggested that "personhood," at least to the extent that it includes a right to life, depends on attributes that are not likely to be developed until sometime after birth. One philosopher has defended infanticide on the grounds that it is indistinguishable from abortion and that neither constitutes the improper killing of a human being because there can be no human being until the being possesses a concept of itself as a continuing subject of experiences and other mental states, and recognizes that it is such a continuing entity. Others have constructed lists of attributes of a person; these attributes might include some kind of basic intelligence, a sense of time and place, an ability to communicate with others, a functioning higher brain, altruism, the ability to feel emotions, and the ability to think logically. Perhaps there is no moment of "personhood;" perhaps we are seeking something that simply does not exist. Perhaps "personhood" is developed through a process over time, and it cannot be identified as attaching at any particular moment.

B. Legal Recognition of Human Life

The law is often forced to confront the question of when rights and privileges of persons attach to fetuses and young children. While children have always been treated differently from adults in the law, those fundamental common law and Constitutional rights that uniformly extend to both competent and incompetent adults also have been extended to children from the time of birth. Courts have had greater difficulty determining which rights, if any, attach to a fetus.

The trend over the past few decades has been for states to expand the common law rights of the fetus and to recognize that the fetus can be an independent victim for purposes of both tort and criminal law. For example, most states now permit a tort action to be filed by an estate of a stillborn child. Just twenty years ago, the vast majority of states required that the child be born alive before any right to sue would attach. Similarly, many states now extend the protection of their homicide law to fetuses; several years ago that extension was very unusual. The extent of any Constitutional protection of fetuses is far less certain.

While the Supreme Court has never formally determined when a fetus becomes a "person" for constitutional purposes, it has not been able to completely avoid that question despite its several attempts to finesse it. Indeed, some commentators thought that the matter was finally resolved in the watershed case of *Roe v. Wade*, when the Court unambiguously announced that "the word 'person,' as used in the Fourteenth Amendment, does not include the unborn." The viability of *Roe* itself has remained uncertain since it was decided in 1973, and, in any case, in the same opinion the Court determined that the state had a legitimate interest in protecting "potential life." The Supreme Court has never determined if there might be some Constitutional limitation on the way that states can define "person" for state law purposes.

State legislatures and courts have addressed the question in a number of ways. Justice Blackmun pointed out in *Roe* that courts have generally considered killing a fetus to be substantially different from killing a person who was born alive. This is reflected in the different penalties that often attach to feticide and other forms of homicide and the fact that feticide itself has been distinguished from murder or manslaughter in many jurisdictions. Over the past several years, however, more and more states have made the penalties for feticide commensurate with the penalties for homicide, and several have promulgated new homicide statutes that explicitly include fetuses as those whose death may give rise to homicide prosecutions.

State courts have confronted this question when determining whether the estate of a fetus has standing to bring a wrongful death action. Historically, courts were divided over whether a live birth was a necessary precedent to a wrongful death action, with several states allowing representatives of viable fetuses as well as representatives of children born alive to bring those actions. There is a certain irony in allowing the mother, often the real beneficiary of any judgment, to recover for the wrongful death of a fetus she was legally entitled to abort. On the other hand, it seems arbitrary to treat a one day old decedent differently from a decedent who was a day away from birth when a tortious act caused the fetus's death. Over the last two decades some courts have allowed wrongful death actions to proceed on behalf of non-viable fetuses, and some courts have set cut-off dates (like quickening) that go back further than viability. There still are limits, though. In 2005 one state supreme court formally rejected a wrongful death claim brought on behalf of a frozen eight cell pre-embryo that had never seen the inside of a womb.

II. ABORTION

A. Introduction

In Roe v. Wade, 410 U.S. 113, 93 S.Ct. 705, 35 L.Ed.2d 147 (1973), the United States Supreme Court recognized the Constitutional right to personal procreative decision making, including the right of a pregnant woman to choose to have an abortion under some circumstances. Justice Blackmun, writing for a 7–2 majority, pored over medical texts and history analyses hoping to find out just when a person protected by the Fourteenth Amendment really did come into existence. He had been counsel to the Mayo Clinic earlier in his legal career and he was keenly aware of the medical consequences of his determination. Further, the right recognized in *Roe* is a right of the pregnant woman which can be exercised only in consultation with her physician. This right recognized in *Roe* was firmly based on the due process clause of the Fourteenth Amendment, not the penumbras and emanations of many provisions of the Bill of Rights, which formed the unstable foundation for Griswold v. Connecticut, 381 U.S. 479, 85 S.Ct. 1678, 14 L.Ed.2d 510 (1965), an earlier case in which the Court found that a married couple had the Constitutional right to use contraceptives. By the time *Roe* was decided, the Supreme Court had already used the Fourteenth Amendment's equal protection clause to extend *Griswold's* protection to unmarried, as well as married, couples.

While *Roe* was increasingly narrowed during the 1980s, and while its death was often predicted, in 1992 the Court concluded that "the essential holding of *Roe v. Wade* should be retained and once again reaffirmed" in Planned Parenthood of Southeastern Pennsylvania v. Casey, 505 U.S. 833, 112 S.Ct. 2791, 120 L.Ed.2d 674 (1992). In Gonzales v. Carhart, 550 U.S. 124, 127 S.C.t. 1610, 167 L.Ed.2d 480 (2007), a case upholding the Constitutionality of the federal Partial Birth Abortion Ban Act, the Supreme Court "assume[d] * * * the principles [of *Roe* and *Casey*] for the purpose of this opinion," although it was not clear that those principles continued to command the respect of the majority of the Court. An understanding of the current Constitutional status of abortion in the United States requires an understanding of these three Supreme Court cases, although even that understanding may not be sufficient to determine the Constitutional future of abortion regulation. The first step, then, is to figure out the "essential holding" of *Roe* that was retained in the *Casey* case and "assumed" in *Carhart*. See Sections B and C, below.

B. *Roe v. Wade*

After reviewing the history of legal regulation of abortion and evaluating the range of contexts in which it is applied, the Court determined that the right to privacy implicit in the Constitution, which the Court found to be based "in the Fourteenth Amendment's concept of personal liberty and restrictions upon state action," was "broad enough to encompass a woman's decision whether or not to terminate her pregnancy." This fundamental right, though, was not absolute. It could be overcome by a compelling state interest. Further, the Court found that there were two state interests that could be compelling—(1) the state interest in protecting the health of the mother, and (2) the state interest in protecting potential life.

The Court then developed the trimester rule which has been the subject of enormous controversy for more than three decades. The state's interest in the health of the mother becomes compelling at the point at which the abortion procedure is more dangerous to the mother than the continued pregnancy. The Court established that point at the end of the first trimester, at least given the available medical techniques in 1973. Thus, under *Roe*, after the first trimester the state is able to regulate abortion for the purposes of protecting the health of the mother. Further, the Court determined that the state's interest in protecting potential life became compelling at the point of viability because at that point the fetus has the "capability of meaningful life outside the mother's womb." The Court established the point of viability, given the medical processes available in 1973, at the end of the second trimester. Thus, the Court determined that during the final trimester the state could limit, or even prohibit, abortion in order to protect the state's interest in the fetus, subject to the caveat that an abortion always had to be available to a woman when it was necessary to preserve her life or her health.

The Court's opinion in *Roe* was vigorously criticized and stirred into action political forces opposed to abortion. They encouraged state legislatures to seek creative ways to discourage abortions without running afoul of the requirements of the case. The Supreme Court at first resisted attempts to limit the underlying rights recognized in 1973, although the number of Justices supporting that decision declined over time. *Roe* was reaffirmed more than a dozen times in its first decade, but by 1986 the 7–2 majority was down to 5–4, and by the end of the 1980s the Court appeared to be evenly divided, with Justice O'Connor unwilling to confront the issue. *Roe* was then reconsidered in *Casey*, which is discussed below.

There were two legal lines of attack on the Supreme Court's decision in *Roe*. The first was that the Supreme Court had returned to the unhappy Lochnerian days of substantive due process, during which the Court acted as if it were free to make social policy without regard to legal or Constitutional restrictions. Of course, the authors of the Fourteenth Amendment were not confronted with abortion as a political and social issue, and the intent of the framers with regard to this particular question is not likely to be helpful in resolving this issue. While the Fourteenth Amendment has been broadly interpreted, *Roe* and the subsequent abortion cases are among the few examples of the application of a "right to privacy" that arise out of that amendment. The Supreme Court has refused to extend this right of privacy to very many other areas, even within the health care system. In 1986 the Supreme Court explicitly rejected the application of the right of privacy to protect those engaging in homosexual conduct in Bowers v. Hardwick, 478 U.S. 186, 106 S.Ct. 2841, 92 L.Ed.2d 140 (1986), and, in a strictly legal, conceptual sense, *Roe v. Wade* appeared to be a derelict on the waters of the law. The vitality of the doctrine of substantive due process was suddenly revived, though, when the Court overturned *Bowers* only seven years after it was decided, in 2003. In Lawrence v. Texas, 539 U.S. 558, 123 S.Ct. 2472, 156 L.Ed.2d 508 (2003), the Court announced that those who engaged in private gay and lesbian sex are protected from criminal action by the state of Texas by the Constitutional right of privacy, which the Court found, once again, firmly rooted in the Due Process Clause of the Fourteenth Amendment.

The second line of attack on *Roe* focused on the opinion's scientific foundation. *Roe* made two kinds of distinctions. First, it identified that point at which it became more dangerous to abort than to bear the child; second, it identified that point at which the fetus was viable. As we have seen, the court identified those points as occurring at the end of the first and second trimesters. As the science of obstetrics improved and safer techniques of abortion developed, the first point moved back, closer to the time of delivery, and the second point moved forward, closer to the time of conception. Soon after *Roe*, it was quite safe to have an abortion long after the end of the first trimester, and a fetus could be viable before the end of the second trimester. The Court had to determine whether it would stick to its scientifically justifiable points (the point of increased danger and the point of viability), which would create some ambiguity because these points would change with the latest medical developments, or whether it would stick with the arbitrary first and second trimester timelines, which are easy to apply, even though they are no longer supported by science. The Court ultimately reconsidered the trimester division altogether in 1992.

C. *Planned Parenthood of Southeastern Pennsylvania v. Casey*

In an opinion jointly authored by Justices O'Connor, Kennedy and Souter, the Court began its opinion in this Constitutional attack on a Pennsylvania statute regulating abortion by saying, directly and conclusively, that "the essential holding of *Roe v. Wade* should be retained and once again reaffirmed." That "essential holding," according to the Court, had three components: (1) the right of a woman to have an abortion before viability "without undue interference" of the government, (2) the right in the state to limit or prohibit an abortion after viability, as long as provision is made to protect the health and safety of the mother, and (3) the recognition that the state interest in protecting both the fetus and the mother commence at the beginning of the pregnancy. The trimester division that played such a large role in *Roe* was not, apparently, a part of its "essential holding," and it was formally abandoned by the Court in *Casey*.

The *Casey* Court provided a new standard to replace the standard used to review statutes regulating abortion for the past two decades: a state limitation on the right to have an abortion is Constitutional as long as it does not impose an "undue burden" on a "woman's ability to make this decision." This "undue burden" standard was to be measured by the "substantial obstacle" test: any state law with the purpose or effect of placing a substantial obstacle in the path of a woman seeking an abortion of a nonviable fetus would constitute an undue burden. From the point of view of the dissenting judges, who would have rejected the entire jurisprudence of *Roe*, the new "undue burden" standard and "substantial obstacle" test were even less Constitutionally defensible than the rule in *Roe*. Chief Justice Rehnquist noted that, despite the language of the majority opinion, there was virtually no part of *Roe* left standing. He called it a "judicial Potemkin village"—an attractive façade, with utterly no substance behind it.

The bewilderment brought on by the "undue burden" analysis was ameliorated by the Court's decisions about particular provisions in the Pennsylvania statute. The Court found that an informed consent requirement, which imposed on physicians an obligation to provide particular information to patients before obtaining their informed consent for an abortion, would not constitute an undue burden as long as the required information were actually true. Similarly, the Court found that the Pennsylvania requirement that all informed consent information about the abortion must be provided to the patient by the doctor, not by any other health care provider or medical office staff, did not constitute an impermissible "undue burden." The same analysis saved the provision in Pennsylvania law that required a 24–hour waiting period between the provision of the statutorily required information to the patient and the performance of the abortion.

The Court also used the "undue burden" analysis to uphold the state requirement that a child seeking an abortion must get the consent of at least one parent, or, if that would be impossible or potentially harmful, the agreement of a state court judge through the statutory "judicial bypass" procedure. The only major provision of the law the Court found to create an "undue burden" on the ability of women to make the decision to have an abortion— to create a "substantial obstacle" in the path of a woman seeking to abort a nonviable fetus—was the provision that required spousal notification before a woman could obtain an abortion. The Court reviewed the terrible consequences that could be faced by women who are obliged to tell their husbands about their planned abortion. The potential physical and devastating psychological abuse, along with the risks of harassment, future violence, loss of financial support, and revelation of the abortion to the family, were enough to make the mandatory notification an undue burden. While the Supreme Court considered a few abortion cases in the years following *Casey*, and while the Court threw out a state law criminalizing partial birth abortion in 2000 using the "undue burden" analysis, when the Court faced the attack on the federal Partial Birth Abortion Ban Act in 2007 after Justice O'Connor had left the Court, the Court was prepared to change the focus of the analysis once again.

D. *Gonzales v. Carhart*

Whatever part of *Roe v. Wade* was left standing after *Casey* was wobbly again after the Court upheld the federal Partial Birth Abortion Ban Act in 2007. While dozens of states had passed acts limiting this particular kind of abortion procedure—the "partial birth abortion"—there was doubt over the validity of those laws after the Supreme Court found the Nebraska partial-birth abortion ban to be unconstitutional in 2000. Nonetheless, Congress passed a slightly modified version of the ban that had been promulgated in many states, and a Constitutional challenge to that Act reached the Supreme Court in 2007. While medical groups argued that this process might be the best medical alternative for some women who had to terminate their pregnancies under some circumstances, the gruesome description of the medical process made it a particularly powerful focus for the debate.

A "dilation and extraction" or "D & E" abortion usually consists of separating the fetus into parts in utero, and then removing the fetus from the uterus through the cervix and the vagina. The process may take many passes, and the fetus is no longer alive by the time that removal is begun. The "D & X," "intact D & E," or "dilation and extraction" procedure, which is also known as a partial birth abortion, uses essentially the same process. In the D & X procedure, though, unlike the very commonly used D & E, the body of the fetus is partially removed from the mother's body, a scissors is placed in the cranium of the fetus and used to spread the skull, and the brain is suctioned out of the skull. This allows the rest of the fetal body to be removed—usually, intact.

The statute makes performing the partial-birth abortion a federal crime unless it is necessary to save the life of the mother. Unlike the Nebraska statute found to be unconstitutional, the federal ban was based on formal findings of Congress (although the Supreme Court majority agreed that some of those findings were patently false). In addition, the criminal provision contained actus reus requirements that went beyond those in the Nebraska statute, as well as a scienter requirement that was never incorporated in the Nebraska statute. The federal ban does not criminalize removing what Justice Kennedy calls an "expired fetus," it criminalizes the act when a doctor "vaginally deliver[s] a living fetus" and then ends its life before removing the full fetus.

The Court decided that the precise language of the federal statute saved it from being unconstitutionally vague or overbroad, and that the statute did not have the Congressional purpose or the effect of putting an undue burden on a woman seeking an abortion because it did not place a substantial obstacle in the path of a woman seeking a late-term previability abortion. In addition, the Court determined that the fact that the statute had an exception to the ban only when the life of the mother, not her health, was at risk was insufficient to find it to violate the Constitution in the course of a facial, rather than as-applied, challenge.

The four dissenting Justices in *Carhart* joined in a strongly worded dissent by Justice Ginsburg, who called the decision "alarming." In addition, Justices Scalia and Thomas concurred in the majority opinion, but they pointed out that they still did not accept the jurisprudence of *Roe*, which gave the Court scrutiny over this issue, which should be left to Congress and the state legislatures. There is no jurisprudentially sound way to square the case throwing out the Nebraska partial-birth abortion act with the *Carhart* case, affirming the Constitutionality of the federal act. More meaningful, perhaps, was the passage of time, the replacement of President Clinton by President Bush, and the replacement of Justice O'Connor by Justice Alito on the Court.

E.   The Future of Abortion

Although it is clear that the Supreme Court is far more tolerant of legislation limiting abortion than it has been over most of the previous 35 years, there may be fewer new cases coming to the Court. First, the change in the administration in Washington in 2009 may yield fewer federal legislative and administrative restrictions on abortion. In addition, the politics of abortion may be in equipoise. For many years after *Roe*, the populist branches of the government were fighting the rule imposed by the Court. With so many restrictions on abortion now part of the law, there may be little political interest in going any further. Most of the politically popular limitations on abortion—like a ban on partial birth abortions, and the requirement that children seeking abortion notify their parents—are already law in most states. Changes to the Supreme Court over the next few years may also bring a different judicial approach.

There are some legal issues that remain unresolved, of course. It is not yet clear whether the undue burden test would be met by a statute that prohibited an abortion for particular purposes, like for gender selection. There also remains some uncertainty over legislation designed to make it difficult to cross a state line to get an abortion that would have been illegal in the first state.

Some issues already addressed by the Court may come back in other forms, too. A one-parent consent or notification requirement is clearly Constitutionally acceptable, but the fate of a two-parent requirement is uncertain. A 24–hour waiting period between consent and abortion is clearly Constitutional, too, but the fate of a two or three or fifteen

day waiting period (also called "two trip requirements" because they require a woman to make two
trips to obtain an abortion) is less certain. States
may also attempt to ban other abortion procedures,
like the currently common D & E procedure, or
impose additional medical requirements on providers who offer abortion services. Finally, the Court
may have to adjudicate the role of federal and state
governments to limit this medical procedure. The
power to regulate abortion seems implicit in the
state police powers, but Congress also may have
this authority through the power conferred by the
commerce clause, as Congress itself claimed in the
text of the Partial Birth Abortion Ban Act. The
Court was not asked to evaluate the power of the
federal government (rather than the power of state
governments) to regulate abortion processes, but it
may in some other context.

III.   POTENTIAL FETAL–MATERNAL CONFLICT

Sometimes courts, and even legislatures, are
called upon to evaluate decisions made by pregnant
women that might be inconsistent with the best
interests of their fetuses. This issue has arisen most
frequently when pregnant women reject medical
advice (such as the advice to have a caesarian
section birth) that a doctor believes is necessary to
preserve the life or health of her fetus. It also arises
when pregnant women decide to engage in certain
behaviors, like using illegal drugs or drinking alco-

hol, that might be dangerous to their fetuses during the pregnancy. Although there has been substantial ethical debate over the propriety of regulating the conduct of pregnant women for the benefit of their fetuses, ultimately the law rarely has intervened to require a physician to treat a pregnant woman in a particular way because that would be best for her fetus.

In the classic case, a physician informs a reluctant pregnant patient that she must have a c-section to allow for her fetus to be born alive and without substantial disabilities that may affect the child for a lifetime, but she still refuses her consent to the c-section. Under the normal rule of informed consent, the competent patient's decision governs. Thus, as long as the pregnant woman is the only patient involved, her decision must govern, even if it is inconsistent with preserving the life of the child who will result from the birth. But is the pregnant woman the only patient?

When a court answers such a question, it must first determine whether it is confronted with a single patient whose decision must govern, or two patients whose interests somehow must be balanced. While the most commonly accepted legal viewpoint is that there is but one patient, and that her decision must be respected, there are many judges and commentators who have suggested that a balancing of the wishes of the pregnant woman and the interests of the fetus is appropriate, at least in some cases. This argument is strongest in a case like the c-section case, when the court is confronted with the imminent birth of the fetus who will then be a child entitled to the respect the law gives to any other human being. The argument for balancing is weakest at the very beginning of the pregnancy, although the state's interest in the life of the fetus has been recognized from the beginning of the pregnancy.

The arguments for balancing get stronger as the fetus develops, and some have argued that balancing is required by the time of viability, when the pregnant woman would no longer have the unconstrained legal option of seeking an abortion. As a general matter, courts only engage in this balancing in "extremely rare and truly exceptional" cases when the clearly established best interests of the fetus are inconsistent with the pregnant woman's choice. Of course, often this balancing will require a court to determine the value of the potentially short and limited life of an extremely ill newborn, and there is simply nothing in law to help judges do that valuation.

The courts that do engage in this balancing must determine which factors can be balanced appropriately. On the one side is the articulated decision of the pregnant woman, who, all recognize, is also likely to be acting in a way she considers best for her fetus. The pregnant woman also has a fundamental interest in making her own healthcare decisions, whether they are morally right or wrong from the perspective of the court. On the same side, generally, is the preservation of the life and health of the mother. On the other side of the scale is the

safe birth of the child with as few birth impairments as is medically possible. Because there is an
element of uncertainty with regard to these factors,
courts may take into account the likelihood that the
consequences feared by each side will actually occur. Courts are increasingly reluctant to depend on
medical predictions that the failure to have a medically supervised birth, like a caesarian section, will
result in harm to the fetus. Doctors have a poor
history of prognosis in these cases, and they seem to
err uniformly on the side of advocating for medical
intervention. If the pregnant woman's decisional
capacity is a matter of uncertainty, the court may
also take that into account by discounting her interest in making her own health care decisions.

Perhaps because the balancing process itself is so
difficult, some advocate balancing the pregnant
woman's interests and the fetus's interests only in
limited circumstances. For example, balancing could
be limited to cases where the fetus is viable, and the
pregnant woman's decision could prevail without
the need for balancing up to that point of the
pregnancy. One scholar has argued that after the
mother has decided to have the child, whenever
that occurs, balancing is required, but before that—
at least as long as the mother also retains the right
to choose to abort the fetus—her decision should
govern without being balanced against any other
interest.

Several states have attempted to apply criminal
law, abuse and neglect law, dependent child law,

civil commitment law, and ordinary tort law to cases where a pregnant woman may put her fetus at risk. For the most part, the state has attempted to intervene in these ways when the pregnant woman is engaging in some unhealthy (and, perhaps, illegal) activity like using illicit drugs or drinking too heavily during pregnancy.

Although more than a dozen states have considered the application of criminal law proscribing homicide, drug abuse, drug distribution, or child abuse and neglect to pregnant women, only one state supreme court ultimately has upheld the conviction of a pregnant woman under these circumstances. The South Carolina Supreme Court affirmed a conviction for homicide by child abuse of a woman whose child was stillborn because of her cocaine use during pregnancy, and that woman is now serving a 20 year sentence. Others have considered drug distribution charges when a pregnant woman passes illegal narcotics to her fetus through the umbilical cord, as well as ordinary homicide and criminal abuse charges. For the most part, courts have rejected the use of the criminal law either because their state law does not include a "fetus" as a "person" or a "child" for statutory purposes, or because the state courts have found it inconsistent with the common law to attach criminal liability to a pregnant woman's conduct that harms her own fetus. Those who support the application of the criminal law in these cases argue that pregnancy and imminent motherhood provide the "teachable moment" that allows criminal law to be most effective in deterring future harmful conduct, while those who oppose it worry that women will not seek prenatal care if that could result in criminal prosecution, and that prosecution of pregnant women for mistreating their fetuses thus will end up doing more harm than good for the fetuses of drug abusing women.

The remedy of civil commitment or court ordered protective custody may be available as an alternative to criminal law to protect fetuses from abuse by mentally ill, drug abusing, or alcoholic mothers under some state laws that permit commitment to treat these conditions. Some states have promulgated statutes that provide that women who put their fetuses at risk may be restrained from doing so by the court. For example, a Wisconsin statute provides that an adult pregnant woman may be held in custody to protect the fetus if there is "a substantial risk that the physical health of the unborn child, and of the child when born, will be seriously affected or endangered by the adult expectant mother's habitual lack of self-control in the use of alcoholic beverages, controlled substances or controlled substance analogs" and "the adult expectant mother . . . has refused to accept any alcohol or other drug abuse services offered to her . . . ." South Dakota has promulgated a similar statute allowing for the brief (two-day) commitment of pregnant women by family members, and court ordered commitment of those same women for up to nine months.

In addition to criminal prosecutions, civil commitment proceedings, and the mandatory injunctions (or their equivalents) that have been sought in the c-section cases, some states allow for separate child protective services actions under state abuse, neglect, "children in need of services," or dependency laws. These laws allow the state to take legal and physical custody of a child in need and to provide the necessary services. Of course, a child protective services agency cannot take physical custody of a fetus under civil abuse and neglect law without also taking custody of the mother, and many states have been reluctant to permit this.

In many high risk pregnancies, though, the pregnant woman is herself a child. In these cases, *her* parents' inability to control her conduct to assure the safety of the fetus may be sufficient to show that the pregnant woman herself is a neglected child, and thus she can be taken into custody to protect her (and, indirectly, her fetus). Finally, civil damages may be available to a child born alive who is injured by the pre-birth conduct of her mother. Mothers have been delighted to allow their children to sue them for pre-birth injuries when there is an insurance company that will pay the damages (sometimes, to the very parent who negligently caused the injury). If a state permits children born alive to seek tort damages against others who injure them prenatally, as most states do, there may be no reason to treat their tortfeasing parents differently and more favorably.

One issue that sometimes arises when there is litigation over a potential fetal-maternal conflict is whether a guardian ad litem should be appointed on behalf of the fetus. Normally a guardian ad litem would be appointed to represent an incompetent person with an interest in particular litigation. But is a fetus such a "person" with a legal interest in the litigation? In some states such guardians ad litem have been appointed as a matter of course; in others, courts have refused to appoint them; and in some, the very appointment has been the subject of ancillary litigation. If one is appointed, the question of what position that guardian ad litem should take also must be resolved.

The guardian ad litem cannot apply the principle of substituted judgment and represent the wishes of the fetus; the concept has no meaning in the context of a fetus. Thus, the guardian ad litem must represent the best interests of the fetus. It is not easy to define those interests, though. Must the guardian ad litem accept the vitalist position that life is always preferable to the alternative, or could a guardian ad litem reasonably argue that in a particular case a fetus who would be born with some serious anomalies and thus lead a short life of terrible suffering would be better off not born at all? Perhaps because of the difficulty in answering these questions, recently judges have erred on the side of not appointing a guardian ad litem when the proposed appointment is the subject of objection.

IV. ASSISTED REPRODUCTIVE TECHNOLOGIES (ART) AND THEIR LEGAL CONSEQUENCES

A. Introduction: The Process of Reproduction

Those seeking medical help in facilitating reproduction do so because they want a child. The birth of a child requires the growth of a fetus in a woman's uterus. This, in turn, requires the implantation of a fertilized ovum in the uterine wall. At least until the cloning of human beings is perfected, the ovum can implant in the uterine wall only if it has been fertilized by a sperm, a process which generally takes place in the fallopian tube.

Within a day of an ovum being fertilized by a sperm, it has divided twice, into a two- and then a four-celled "embryo" (sometimes called a "preembryo," and sometimes still called a "fertilized ovum"). Some will argue that because there is no differentiated living matter yet (i.e., there are no fetal or placental cells yet), this division of cell material is not a constructive development of living substance. It is a process which does nothing to distribute particular developmental qualities to particular parts of a resulting fetus. On the other hand, it is the preliminary stage which makes it possible for the embryo—or whatever it may be called—to implant and use materials from the uterine wall to grow and develop into a fetus. Obviously, the fertilization of the ovum by the sperm begins the em-

bryonic process, although some use the term "embryo" only to apply to later stages of development.

At any rate, whether it is called an embryo, a pre-
embryo, a fertilized ovum, or something else, it
continues its migration through the fallopian tube
toward the uterus. The fertilized and subdividing
ovum arrives at the lower end of the fallopian tube,
hesitating for about two days before being expelled
into the uterus. This delay allows the uterine lining
to build itself up for successful implantation. The
implantation of this cell cluster is a complicated
biological process that takes several days.

Even when all other conditions are met, not all
fertilized ova actually do implant and not all implanted ova survive until birth. About 50% of fertilized ova are expelled from the body before the
woman has any reason to know that she is pregnant. Some of these spontaneous expulsions occur
before implantation, and some occur during the
first few days after the commencement of the implantation process.

There are several reasons that those who wish to
raise children may not conceive them through this
natural process. First, some are unable to participate in coital sexual relations, or choose not to
participate in such relations. Others are infertile—
that is, normal coitus does not result in a fertilized
ovum that implants in the uterine wall and grows
into a fetus and then a child. Although estimates
vary, at least 10% of American couples are infertile.
There are a variety of reasons for infertility. Some

men do not produce sperm that is capable of fertilizing the ovum. Some women are unable to produce
ova, for example, and others have fallopian tubes
that cannot adequately accept ova to be fertilized,
or do not permit the travel of fertilized ova to the
uterus. In some cases, the "shell" around the ovum
may not admit any sperm at all. In other cases, the
ovum is successfully fertilized but the uterus is
incapable of allowing for implantation of the fertilized ovum or of maintaining the implanted embryo
through the pregnancy. In all of these cases, some
form of intervention may allow those who could not
become parents through unassisted coitus to
achieve parenthood nonetheless.

The range of problems that prevent conception
and child-bearing give rise to a wide variety of
alternative interventions. These interventions, in
turn, require the involvement of a host of other
people. A sperm source (who is often a sperm ven-
dor rather than a sperm donor) is necessary where
the problem is the lack of a man or a man's inability to produce physiologically adequate sperm; an
ovum source is necessary where the problem is a
woman's inability to provide a potentially fertile
ovum; a uterus source (originally called a "surrogate mother," now more generally described as a
"gestational mother" or a "gestational surrogate")
is necessary where a woman is unable or unwilling
to carry the fertilized ovum through the pregnancy
in her own uterus. Medical treatment of an ovum
may allow it to be fertilized, and treatment of a
fertilized ovum may allow it to be implanted. Some-

times a combination of these needs requires that there be a series of interventions to produce a pregnancy and a child. A woman may be unable to produce ova and unable to carry a fertilized ovum in her uterus, for example. There may be several options available to allow her to obtain both an ovum that can be fertilized (from an ovum source) and a uterus for the gestation of that fertilized ovum (from a gestational mother).

The processes that give rise to these issues include AIH (artificial insemination-homologous, that is, artificial insemination of a woman with the sperm of the person who is intended to be the biological and nurturing father, often the husband), AID (artificial insemination-donor, that is, artificial insemination of the woman with the sperm of someone who is presumed to have no continuing relationship with the child), IVF (in vitro fertilization, that is, fertilizing an ovum outside of the uterus and then implanting it), embryo transfer, egg transfer, and gestational surrogacy (carrying a fetus expected to be raised by an identifiable person other than the pregnant woman). There are other techniques that may be applied to aid fertilization problems—such as full IVP (in vitro pregnancy, that is, an artificial womb maintained in a medical facility) and cloning—but these are unlikely to be of much practical concern over the next few years. There are hundreds of thousands of children now alive in the United States who were conceived by AID; there are tens of thousands who are the result of in vitro fertilization, and thousands carried by surrogate mothers. Questions surrounding their legal status are real, substantial, and immediate.

B.   The Legal Questions

The hardest social and legal question arising out of the use of assisted reproductive techniques may be identifying the parents of the resulting children. The law must determine the parents of each child, and it must determine the rights and obligations that attach to each of those parents. That makes the determination of parentage a very important decision, of course, but courts and legislatures have been forced to face other issues, too, like the status of gametes (like sperm and ova) and embryos that have not been implanted in any uterus. Are they tiny people, or pieces of property owned by others, or something different from either of those?

It is not hard to imagine the variety of unusual legal relationships which can develop as a consequence of medical and non-medical reproductive techniques. It is possible to have a child who is the product of sperm from one source (whose sperm may be mixed with sperm from several sources), an ovum extracted from one woman, implanted in another, and carried for the benefit of yet another set of parents who intend to nurture the child from the time of its birth. We are concerned about the use of new technology to facilitate reproduction in part because of its potential effect on family structure, and because any change in family structure may also have an impact on our social structure.

Over the last century American social living arrangements, and the consequent notions of the family, have become even more uncertain. Last century a society of extended families (which were extended both horizontally, to include near relatives, and vertically, to include near generations) was transformed through increased mobility, increased urbanization, and increased industrialization into a society of nuclear families, each family possessing an identifiable head of a household (generally the father) a mother, and children; the dog was optional. Over the past few decades, this model of the family has been tested by many forces, including those that come from women's reassessment of their roles. Even greater changes have driven us from a society of nuclear families to a society of "constructed" families—designer families, really—where relationships between adults, and between adults and children, are arranged on an ad hoc basis or by agreement, whether it be a formal contract or a set of unarticulated expectations. While many of these new "constructed" families look very much like the families of the past, many do not. Many are one-parent families, some include more than two parents, some include two parents of the same gender, and in some families a generation is skipped, leaving grandparents to raise their grandchildren.

The law has struggled to deal with the social and medical developments that made these families possible with only limited success. While courts have been able to develop processes to accommodate the breakup of nuclear families—custody and support arrangements, primarily—neither the courts nor legislatures have done very well in developing institutions that are capable of dealing with these previously legally unrecognized families. Ultimately this society will call upon the law to define families, declare family relationships, and allocate power within families.

1.   Artificial Insemination, In Vitro Fertilization, and the Question of Parentage

Artificial insemination is the placement of the semen in the vagina (or in the cervical canal) by means other than the penis. Usually, the sperm is put into a syringe and injected directly into the woman who intends to become pregnant. This process, using "fresh" semen, need not be a medical procedure; it can be done successfully at home by anyone who understands the underlying biological principles. Ideally, the insemination is done at about the time of ovulation, a time that can be determined with increasing accuracy through home ovulation prediction tests.

Medically performed artificial insemination now generally employs frozen semen rather than fresh semen. Although freezing semen permits subsequent tests upon the donor to determine the presence of some latent contaminant (HIV, for example, or some genetic defect), the freezing process is comparatively difficult and expensive. The semen is mixed with a preservative before it is frozen, and it must be carefully thawed before it is used. Once the semen is frozen, however, it is unlikely to undergo substantial deterioration; one estimate is that the risk of genetic mutation will double if the semen is kept frozen for 5,000 years.

Virtually no legal questions have arisen surrounding a wife's use of her husband's sperm to conceive, even if the sperm is artificially injected into the vagina or cervical canal. Such a process may be used within a marriage to allow for processing of the semen to overcome low sperm count. In these cases, there is no question about the identity of the mother and the father of the child. While there are some religious objections to masturbation (which is required) and to any process that alters the "natural" arrangement, artificial insemination of a married woman with sperm from her husband has now become well accepted as a social and medical matter, and it is not a matter of substantial legal concern.

When the sperm is not that of the husband of the woman whose pregnancy results, the question of who ought to be considered the father of the resulting child may arise. For the most part this matter has been resolved by the adoption of the 1973 Uniform Parentage Act (adopted, at least in part, in one form or another, in most states). In 2000 the original (1973) Uniform Parentage Act and the subsequent Uniform Status of Children of Assisted Conception Act were combined and rewritten in the form of a new (2000) Uniform Parentage Act, which was amended in 2002. The portions of this new statute that deal with assisted reproduction have proven highly controversial, and only a few states have adopted substantial parts of the new Uniform Parentage Act. The 1973 Uniform Parentage Act applies only when a wife is artificially inseminated by a physician with the written consent of her husband. Under those circumstances, the husband is the legal father of the child, and the sperm source has no legal relationship with the child. The most recent version of this Uniform Act, in a provision that specifically exempts surrogacy cases, provides that a "donor" is not a parent of a child conceived by means of assisted reproduction unless the donor is the husband of the woman inseminated, or either (1) the man and woman have signed an agreement describing their intended parentage or (2) the man and woman reside together and hold the child out as theirs during the first two years of the child's life. This version of the Uniform Act also provides that a woman can become a mother of a child by giving birth, by adjudication, or by adoption. A father can become a parent by an unrebutted presumption of paternity, a legally effective acknowledgment of paternity, adoption, or the provision of sperm to artificially inseminate his wife.

The parentage questions may get slightly more complicated when a pregnancy arises as a result of in vitro fertilization. In vitro (literally, "in glass") fertilization is a highly technical medical intervention. In the normal in vitro case, an ovum that is ready to be released from the ovary is identified through laparoscopy or ultrasound and removed from the ovary by surgery or aspiration through a hollow needle. The ovum (or ova—there usually is an attempt to get several) is placed in a container with the appropriate amount of semen containing fertile sperm. The fertilized ovum is then placed in the woman's uterus, where it is permitted to implant and develop.

Because the chances of success are increased if several fertilized ova are returned to the uterus, and because of the high cost and physical burden of repeating the procedure, women undergoing in vitro fertilization are generally given drugs to increase the number of ova that become ripe and ready for release and fertilization in one cycle. If there are more retrieved ova, there is a greater chance to develop a fertilized ovum in vitro. Further, in the United States clinics generally try to deliver a few fertilized ova to the uterus simultaneously to assure that at least one will develop. While "superovulation" and the process of harvesting several ova increases the chances of successful fertilization and implantation, inducing ovulation itself has adverse side effects. In addition, the simultaneous placement of multiple fertilized ova results in a higher rate of multiple births than in the rest of the population. These factors give rise to legal problems surrounding the selective reduction of multiple embryos (which some consider to be abortion) when they all start developing in the uterus. In addition, these factors give rise to concerns over the appropriate disposition of those fertilized ova that are not implanted. The legal issues that arise out of in vitro fertilization multiply when the fertilized ova are placed in a woman other than the one who produced them. In such a case, the pregnant woman is not the genetic mother of the child that she is carrying. Of course, the man expecting to raise the child may not be the genetic father either.

In vitro fertilization using the ova of a woman into whom they are replaced and the sperm of that woman's husband raise no more moral or legal questions, at least as to the status of the parents, than AIH. Analogously, in vitro fertilization using the ova supplied by the woman into whose womb they are returned and the sperm of a man not her husband ought to be treated very much like AID, at least as regards the status of the parents. Parentage in uncontested versions of these cases is usually pretty simple to establish because it is consistent with the two traditional rules of parentage: (1) the parents are the ones who provided gametes for their children, and (2) the mother is the one who gave birth to her child.

The courts have had a harder time dealing with cases where those who seek to be treated as parents are not the source of the sperm or the ova. What happens when gametes from two "donors" are combined and implanted in the uterus of a woman who intends to raise the consequent babies with her partner? It is rare for a state to have a clear and unambiguous statute that answers this question, although in some states statutes can be the starting point for the analysis. Generally, the courts must look elsewhere for principles that help resolve these questions.

The courts have addressed several different potentially governing legal rules with regard to identifying the parents of a child resulting from assisted reproduction. First, genetic essentialism, the principle that says that a child's genetic progenitors are that child's parents, has a very strong grip on the way our scientific generation views parentage. If there is no governing statute, courts will often look to that principle as a default position. On the other hand, this society recognizes that such an approach is not always appropriate, and the law allows for the adoption of children and the termination of parental rights in some, albeit limited, circumstances. Even those cases that permit the termination of parental rights, though, often begin with an assumption of parentage in the genetic contributors.

Recently the genetic essentialist position has been challenged by the principle that those whose planning led to the creation of the child—those who intended to be the parents when the process began—ought to be recognized as the parents. This "intent of the parties" approach recognizes the parents who made all the arrangements as the but-for cause of the existence of the child. In a society that recognizes the substantial value that many people put on being a parent, it would make sense to apply the "intent of the parties" principle to encourage those potential parents to engage in the investment and preparation necessary to bring a child of assisted reproduction into being.

Although the law has moved toward accepting this principle, it has also placed limits on its use. No state yet allows more than two people to act as legal parents of a child, and some states require that one of those parents be a man and the other a woman. It may take a village to raise a child, but, apparently, not all villagers are eligible for the status of parent. Indeed, some argue that if the organizers of an IVF birth get a chance to choose the parents by contract, the organizers of a birth resulting from coitus ought to be able to do so, too. Why should the progenitor or the womb source automatically be presumed to be a parent? Of course, this would require a dramatic change from the current, essentially biological, principles of family law that are used to determine parentage in such cases

Some judges have also asked what would be best for the potential children, and those judges would resolve the parentage question by applying a "child's best interest" analysis. This is a novel application of that principle, though, since it has been applied historically only when (1) there are disputes between parents, (2) there are no potential parents available, or (3) it can be applied as one factor when the state acts to terminate parental rights. There are many children whose parentage is clear but whose best interest, alas, would be served by the replacement of their current parents by other, better, ones.

In a great deal of the increasingly routine litigation over children born as a result of assisted reproductive technologies the courts have been confront-

ed with two very different forms of legal analysis:
the cases can be seen as parentage cases in the mold
of old fashioned paternity actions, or they can be
seen as cases that are analogous to adoption actions. The first approach makes both the genetic
essentialist and the "intent of the parties" theories
particularly attractive, while the second may cause
the court to focus on the best interest of the child.
In addition, the first approach allows the court to
determine parentage without restraint, while the
second presumes there was some set of original
parents, even if their identity is undetermined, who
are to be replaced by the newly adjudicated parents.
Increasingly, state courts are seeing the issues as
sui generis, as different from ordinary paternity
actions as they are from ordinary adoption cases.

While the starting point of much of the state
courts' legal analysis of parentage in assisted reproduction cases must be state statutes, that is not
always the heart of the debate. Courts have routinely considered equal protection and due process arguments, raised under both the state and the United States constitutions. While courts have generally
rejected the equal protection argument that a sperm
provider has to be treated like an ova provider or a
woman carrying a pregnancy, the symmetry between them has been recognized in some cases. The
argument that the state would deny a parent due
process by failing to recognize a parent-child relationship usually starts with the assumption of parentage. There is a due process liberty interest in
being a parent—there is no doubt about that—but

that interest only attaches when the parental relationship already has been established. It would be circular to recognize a parental relationship because failing to do so would impose a burden on the liberty interest of a parent.

In addition to establishing the parentage of a child of assisted reproduction, courts have been called upon to determine the status, and the appropriate disposition, of sperm, ova, and, most significantly, the fertilized ova which are often cryogenically preserved with the knowledge that the progenitors may decide to use them to create subsequent pregnancies.

2.   The Question of the Status of "Extra" Fertilized Ova

There are often fertilized ova that remain unimplanted following the application of assisted reproductive techniques. These fertilized ova are much more easily cryogenically preserved than unfertilized ova, and they may be saved for future use by the parties or others. At some point, though, the law must consider how to dispose of them. Courts have had a great deal of trouble addressing this question of disposition because they are uncertain of the status of these fertilized ova.

Perhaps because of the problems with all of the alternatives, courts have often recognized any prior arrangement for the disposition of the fertilized ova that the sperm and ova sources agreed upon by contract. Most fertility clinics now include a provision for the disposition in their form contracts, although that disposition varies. The default position appears to be cryogenically preserving the pre-embryos until the parties are sure that they will not use them, and then donating the pre-embryos for research, donating the pre-embryos for use by other infertile couples who need them, or thawing and destroying the fertilized ova. The courts often look for an unambiguous statement of intent from the parties, and that is clearest in a signed, written contract.

In the absence of a contract—or, in some states, in the face of an inconsistent contract—the courts must apply other principles to determine the disposition of the pre-embryos, an issue that arises fairly commonly when a couple going through IVF breaks up. The pre-embryos could be considered personal property of the couple—much like the couple's sofa or their pet macaw—and be distributed according to the ordinary laws of property, as they would be in the course of a separation agreement or a divorce. If a domestic relations court is unsure what to do with the six bar stools, it can simply award three to each party. If there are a dozen remaining fertilized ova, each progenitor could be awarded six, to use or destroy as that progenitor sees fit. This raises substantial problems, though, because these items of property are more significant for what they may become than for what they are.

Instead, pre-embryos could be treated like the human beings they have the capacity to become rather than mere property, and at least one state requires this as a matter of statute. If they are treated as human beings—as a kind of very young child—courts would routinely apply the best interest standard to determine which of the parents should be awarded custody. Some courts would assume that the party most likely to arrange to have the pre-embryos brought to term would be the one serving the best interest of the child/fertilized ova. The problem with this resolution of the disposition problem is that it is inconsistent with the principle, recognized by some courts, that no one should be forced into parentage against that person's wishes. Awarding a dozen left over fertilized ova to the sperm source because he promises to distribute them to infertile couples would require his former partner, the source of the ova, to become mother of a dozen children who could be raised by a dozen other mothers and fathers, and that seems unfair to her.

Just as courts are reluctant to force parenthood on a person who no longer wants it by requiring the implantation of a pre-embryo that a progenitor no longer wants to see developed, courts are sympathetic to the requests of potential parents who are otherwise infertile. Those courts which have recognized a Constitutional right not to become a parent also recognize that such a right may have to give way to the right of a progenitor to become a parent when use of the fertilized ova is that person's only chance. When one of the parties is no longer fertile, even with the assistance of IVF and other ART techniques, courts have been open to the idea of awarding that infertile partner some of his or her own pre-embryos for implantation, even when the other progenitor opposes it.

There are some other principles that could be used to dispose of frozen pre-embryos. Some have argued that the ova source should always be awarded the pre-embryos. First, it is much harder on the woman to have her ova superstimulated and harvested than it is on the man to provide sperm. Her investment in the process is so much greater, the argument goes, that she ought to end up with the final product. Second, a fertilized ova with the capacity to develop into a human being is not really different from a fetus in the womb. Principles of abortion law provide that the woman (and not the male progenitor) has virtually plenary control over the fetus—up to and including the right to abort that fetus during some part of the pregnancy—and thus the woman must have that same authority over the fertilized ova, which are essentially unimplanted fetuses. Others argue that it devalues parentage altogether and insures a difficult childhood to the child to award pre-embryos to one or another fighting progenitor, and, absent an alternative agreement at the time of the disposition, the default position should be that all fertilized ova should be destroyed when the original arrangements fail. In fact, in some countries, "extra" fertilized embryos are automatically destroyed after some established period of time following the last attempt at implantation. Other suggestions for disposing of fertilized ova include making them available to anyone who will gestate them, or distributing them to laboratories doing stem cell research, where they have substantial scientific value.

The law surrounding the disposition of pre-embryos remains uncertain. They do not seem to fit neatly into the category of personal property, and legal principles that apply there are not routinely applied to pre-embryos. They also do not fit neatly into the category of human beings, so the legal principle normally applied to the disposition of children—the best interest standard—does not seem to work well, either. Perhaps because of this uncertainty, courts seem to be increasingly willing to adhere to agreements that the parties made with regard to the fertilized ova, although courts are keenly cognizant of the important Constitutional and common law rights of individuals both to become parents, and to avoid having parenthood thrust upon them.

3. Surrogacy

Surrogacy may be the least technological of reproductive technologies. It is also the oldest: Genesis tells of Abraham's servant Hagar bearing a child to be raised by the genetic father, Abraham, and his wife Sarah. Surrogacy is that arrangement in which a woman carries a child to term intending at the initiation of the pregnancy for another woman to raise the child as the social mother. As was the case with Hagar, fertilization may take place through normal coitus and result in "natural surrogacy." It also may be a consequence of artificial insemination, in vitro fertilization or embryo transfer. While the genetic father may be the husband of the woman who expects to raise the child as its mother, that need not be the case. While the genetic mother is often the pregnant woman, that is not required either; an arrangement in which the pregnant woman is not the source of the ovum is called gestational surrogacy. It is not only possible to take the sperm from one source, the ovum from another and place the subsequently developed embryo in the uterus of a third person, it has become fairly common.

Although there is some debate about whether surrogacy ought to be considered a "medical treatment" for infertility, it provides the only way for a woman without a uterus to be the genetic mother of a child (through embryo transfer, for example), or to be the mother of a child whose genetic father is her partner (through artificial insemination of the surrogate with the partner's sperm). In addition, some women may choose to avoid pregnancy because it poses grave physical or emotional risk to them, or because it would be difficult for them to continue to work (or play) while pregnant.

Commercial surrogacy arrangements have given rise to a great deal of controversy. While the newest version of the Uniform Parentage Act includes an article recognizing surrogacy contracts and regulating them, that provision has not proven popular in state legislatures. More often, state courts have

been called upon to determine whether such contracts should be legal and enforceable, criminal and
void ab initio, or something in between—for example, legal (i.e., not criminal) but still not enforceable. About a dozen state courts have judicially
recognized surrogacy contracts, although some have
placed limitations and restrictions on them. Surrogacy contracts also have been rejected by some
courts. Some states have outlawed such contracts
absolutely, generally by statute. Yet other states
allow surrogacy contracts, but only if there is no
payment to the gestational surrogate. When there is
no governing statute, a dispute between the parties
will require the courts to determine the rights and
responsibilities of all of those involved, and the
propriety and enforceability of any contractual arrangements of the parties.

Most of the ethical arguments against surrogacy
fall into three categories—those related to the contracting parties, those related to the child, and
those related to the effect of the process on society
as a whole. The first argument generally advanced
against surrogacy is that it exploits women who are
willing to give or rent their bodies as vessels to
carry other people's children. Essentially, those who
take this view argue that the inducement of substantial payment for pregnancy may cause a woman
to consent to something that otherwise would be an
unthinkable intrusion upon her body. The development of commercial surrogacy, this argument continues, could lead to a class of poor women who will
become child-bearers for wealthy women who do

not want to spend the time or energy on pregnancy. Further, the fact that there is a relationship between ethnicity and the distribution of wealth in this society could mean that we will develop separate child-bearing races and child-raising races. Indeed, over the last few years there is no question that many Americans seeking children have "outsourced" pregnancy to women in India, where the cost of labor, quite literally, is far cheaper than it is in the United States.

Feminists are divided on this issue. Some are deeply offended by the overt use of the woman's body that is the whole goal of a surrogacy arrangement; others believe it is merely misguided paternalism that leads courts (and others) to conclude that women are incapable of deciding for themselves whether they should enter surrogacy contracts. Some economists argue that making surrogacy contracts unenforceable merely lowers the amount that is paid to surrogates. Thus, they suggest, making surrogacy contracts unenforceable is just another in a long history of allegedly protectionist regulations that, in reality, restrict what a woman may choose to do with her body.

Some argue that surrogacy contracts ought to be prohibited or discouraged because they advance only the best interests of the contracting parties, not the best interests of the child. Normally in a custody dispute between those with claims as parents, the court will look to the best interests of the child in determining the appropriate placement. Enforcing a surrogacy contract is necessarily inconsistent with this principle. In addition, some believe that children who find out that they were carried by a surrogate will be injured by that discovery; and others argue that surrogacy contracts render children instruments for the use of parents, not ends in themselves, and that this is necessarily harmful for children.

Finally, some believe that the fabric of society as a whole is weakened by surrogacy arrangements, at least commercial ones. As one state supreme court justice put it in an early surrogacy case, there are some things that money cannot (and should not be able to) buy.

The legal arguments made against recognizing explicit or implicit surrogacy arrangements are parallel to the ethical arguments. Both sides cite a host of federal and state constitutional rights, from the right to privacy and the right to procreate to the clearly established Constitutional right to make family decisions. Those who oppose surrogacy arrangements also argue that they undermine state statutes that limit the circumstances that justify removing a child from the child's natural family.

They also argue that commercial surrogacy contracts violate statutes outlawing baby selling, which is illegal in every state. There is, however, confusion over the original purpose of statutes that prohibit baby selling. They may be intended to protect parents from financial inducements to give up their children (and thus designed to help parents), or they may be intended to protect children from being reduced to the status of an ordinary commodity (and thus designed to protect children). Both may be anachronistic justifications for the entry of the state into this kind of decision making, and some economists have argued that children might do better if they are raised by people who were willing to spend large sums for them rather than by parents who are willing to sell them.

Some have argued that a surrogacy contract, which is a contract to put one's body to work for the benefit of another, is nothing more than a form of slavery. The Thirteenth Amendment prohibits contracts for slavery, even if the contracting parties are all competent adults who are acting voluntarily. One argument for the Thirteenth Amendment itself is that in addition to whatever it offers those who might be or become slaves, society as a whole is better off if the status of "slave" is impossible for everyone. Perhaps all people in this society—including those who would never participate in a surrogacy contract in any way—are better off if the society simply eliminates the possibility of these contracts.

In the absence of any governing state law, the courts will be called upon to determine who have the rights and obligations of parents with regard to a child born as the result of a surrogacy arrangement. Historically, at least determining who is the mother has been fairly easy. The mother is the one who gave birth to the child, who is also the female contributor of genetic material, and, usually, one of those who engaged in conduct which set the whole process in motion. Now, however, those can all be different people—the genetic material in the ova can come from one source and it can be implanted in the uterus of another woman as the result of an arrangement set up by yet a third potential mother. In such cases, the courts must reconsider the question of establishing motherhood.

Increasingly courts are looking to the intent of the parties, at least as a tie-breaker when two women make a claim of motherhood, one based on genetics and one based on gestation. Where it is clear that all of the parties intended the child to be raised by an identifiable mother, through the provision of a contract, for example, that person is increasingly deemed to be the mother whether she is the ovum source or the gestational mother. Some judges, rejecting this intent test as a tie-breaker, would choose another principle of family law discussed above—the best interest test—and allow the court to declare the one who can best mother the child to be the legal mother, at least among those with some biological claim.

One solution to this quandary may be found in the new Uniform Parentage Act surrogacy provision, which would allow those who wish to enter surrogacy contracts to seek their approval by the court before they are executed. This section of the new Uniform Parentage Act authorizes the court to issue an "order validating the gestational agreement." If the court has issued a validating order and a baby is born as a result of the arrangement, the court will issue an order confirming the intending parents as the child's legal parents, granting them physical and legal custody, and ordering the state to list them as the parents on the birth certificate.

The new Uniform Parentage Act takes strong positions on a number of controversial issues: the drafters declare that surrogacy contracts are legally acceptable, that the surrogate may be reasonably compensated for her labor, that judicial approval is necessary before such an agreement can be enforced (and that non-approved contracts are not enforceable, but not illegal, either), and that the intending parents must undergo a home study that shows them "suitable" to be an adopting family. The proposed statute has made little headway in statehouses around the country, though.

The legal approach to the regulation of gestational agreements (and to assisted reproduction more generally) depends on the legal perspective one brings to the enterprise. Family lawyers tend to view the process as analogous to adoption, and they ask how any proposed regulation ought to be different from the regulation that governs adoption. The 2002 version of the Uniform Parentage Act, which requires a home study before a surrogacy arrangement is permitted and places a great deal of authority in the judge, is based on this adoption approach to ART. Health lawyers are more likely to see the process as the provision of a form of health care, and they ask how regulation designed to assure the quality of our health care system can best be applied to help "patients" in this area achieve their goal—usually, parentage of a child. Informed consent requirements—everything from providing infertility center success rates to the potential physical consequences of being a surrogate—seem to come out of a health care-based approach to ART. Criminal lawyers are more likely to ask whether there is any aspect of assisted reproductive techniques that should be prohibited. Attempts to make the whole process illegal come out of this criminal law approach to the issue. As a society, we have not reached a consensus on whether the creation of a child through the use of assisted reproduction techniques, including surrogacy, is more like ordinary procreation (for which we do not require marriage, a home study, "parental fitness," or advance judicial approval), or adoption. It is not surprising that the ambivalence of the courts reflects the ambivalence of the rest of the society.

4. ART and the Law of Marriage

The technology for facilitating reproduction is of special interest to single men and women, and to same sex couples. The use of a surrogate is the only way that a single man could expect to have a child to whom he would be genetically related. Similarly, the use of artificial insemination may be an especially attractive way for a single woman, or a lesbian couple, to have a child. While the law has put no formal restriction on the availability of reproductive techniques, some physicians and clinics have refused to provide the full range of infertility services to single people or non-traditional families. In California, the state supreme court has determined that local and state statutes restricting discrimination on the basis of sexual preference or marriage status can provide avenues of relief for gay and lesbian potential parents who are denied reproductive services for this reason.

Parents in same sex couples also face special problems when their relationships end. The rules for the formation of families vary from state to state, of course, and what is permitted in some states is inconsistent with fundamental state policy in others. In addition, the law defining who is recognized as a parent in one state may be inconsistent with the law of parentage in another. This can create particularly difficult problems when the courts of one state are asked to give full faith and credit, as is required by the Constitution, to the parentage, custody, and child support determinations of another state that has a very different law of marriage. This is made even more complicated by the Federal Defense of Marriage Act ("DOMA"), which provides that a state need not give full faith and credit to a decision of another state "respecting a relationship between persons of the same sex that is treated as a marriage...." It is unclear whether this means that a state need not recognize parentage when that parentage is based on a marital relationship that is recognized in the partners' home state but not elsewhere. The Constitutional status of DOMA is currently the subject of litigation.

C. Cloning

In 1997 the world was stunned by the revelation that a Scottish laboratory had cloned a mammal—to be precise, a Finn Dorset sheep. Scientists achieved this by removing the nucleus from a sheep ovum, replacing it with the genetic material from the sheep to be cloned, and then reimplanting the genetically changed ovum back into the surrogate mother sheep. In fact, the one cloned sheep was the only success in almost 300 attempts, and scientists warned that the likelihood that this technology would be available for human beings remained, for the present, several years away. Despite this, the bioethics community began a world-wide discussion on the consequences of cloning as a form of human reproduction.

Is it possible to talk about the creation of human beings through cloning as we talk about the creation of human beings through other processes of assisted reproduction? Cloning requires in vitro manipulation (like in vitro fertilization) and then implantation in a womb (like surrogacy), so the legal analysis of the cloning process may bear some relationship to the legal analysis we apply otherwise to ART. It is different from either of those two forms of assisted reproduction, though, and it creates a new set of related individuals who cannot be simply described as parents, siblings, or, perhaps, anything other than "precursors" or "antecedents." Some suggest that cloning is not really a form of reproduction at all, but, rather, something different—

perhaps, merely replication. There is much that we cannot predict about a society with cloned human members, but we do know that if human beings are created through cloning, the law will be called upon to determine the formal relationships among the parties.

For generations, science fiction has raised fears of totalitarian regimes that can clone human beings for slave-like work for the benefit of the regime. Cloning could be appropriated by the state in support of a totalitarian eugenics policy, of course, but then so could other currently available reproductive techniques. A related worry is that a society could treat a newly cloned person as nothing more than the continuation of the source of its genetic material—or as a body parts source for the person who provided the genetic material. The law would have to determine if a cloned person has all of the rights of any other person. As some bioethicists argue, if our society were to treat cloned human beings as slaves or spare parts warehouses, the existence of cloning would be the least of our problems.

Cloned people could be treated like identical twins. Identical twins have a common genetic make-up, as a clone and his source would, yet we treat those twins as separate human beings with separate lives and we have identified no social dislocation that arises out of their existence. Perhaps we should be no more worried about cloned human beings than about identical twins. In fact, because a cloned person and his source would be different ages, they would be likely to be raised in different environments, and thus to be less similar than identical twins. On the other hand, the number of identical twins is naturally limited, and there are very few identical triplets. We could, through cloning, create a much larger number of identical "siblings."

Although there may be no good reason for cloning a full human being in the first place, a few possible scenarios that could justify cloning have been put forward. Suppose a child were dying of a disease that could be treated with a bone marrow transplant from a genetically identical donor, but such a donor could not be found. It might be acceptable to clone the patient, and then, independently, determine if the newly replicated person ought to be a donor for his brother. Alternatively, if a couple has an infertility problem which makes it impossible for either of them to become a parent in the ordinary course of events, perhaps they should be able to opt for cloning so that their child will be related to one of them?

This issue has become more complicated because human reproduction is not the only goal of cloning. Cloning of human stem cells may also be useful in developing therapies for medical conditions that are now untreatable. Many view cloning with the intent of creating a new human being—*reproductive cloning*—as posing far more ethical and legal difficulty than cloning human stem cells with the intent to research or create a medical treatment—*therapeutic cloning*.

Both forms of cloning generally require somatic cell nuclear transfer, the process used to create Dolly the cloned sheep. The resulting ovum cell, which has the full complement of human genetic material, is then stimulated so that it will divide and form a pre-embryo. In *therapeutic cloning*, some cells from the pre-embryo are removed for purposes of medical research or treatment. These stem cells have the potential to develop into almost any human cells, and they may be useful in repairing almost any human tissue. Once those cells are removed, though, the pre-embryo cannot develop into a human being. In *reproductive cloning*, the pre-embryo would be placed in a uterus to develop into a human being.

Several national and state bioethics commissions, task forces, and advisory boards have considered the ethics of both reproductive and therapeutic cloning to evaluate the need for legal regulation. While there is a consensus that we should be concerned about potential safety problems in reproductive cloning, there is disagreement over everything else. Some believe that reproductive cloning should be an option available, at least to some people under some circumstances; others argue that this unnatural and potentially dangerous and socially disruptive process is never morally tolerable. Some believe that therapeutic cloning to produce stem cells for medical research is not only permitted, but is morally required to help those suffering from diseases we may be able to conquer, while others conclude that creating a fertilized ovum for the purpose of destroying it and using it for another person's benefit is inherently morally wrong.

The national debate over both reproductive and therapeutic cloning has been reflected in the state legislatures and in Congress. Some states have acted to outlaw human cloning for reproductive purposes, and some appear to have outlawed it for any purpose, including stem cell research. On the other hand, some states have appropriated funds for research involving stem cells, with the assumption that such research will depend upon therapeutic cloning. See Section VII in Chapter 8.

The international debate on cloning parallels the debate in the United States. In 2005, the United Nations General Assembly faced conflicting conventions that would ban either reproductive cloning or all cloning. Ultimately, the General Assembly adopted a resolution encouraging member nations to ban cloning that is "incompatible with human dignity and the protection of human life," whatever that may mean. Many countries fund and encourage stem cell research, some ban it outright, and others allow such research under relatively strict government regulation.

CHAPTER 3

GENETICS

I. INTRODUCTION

In the nineteenth century, Gregor Mendel, an Austrian monk known as the "Father of Genetics," mapped the pathway of genes in the phenotypes (or appearances) of plants. Even earlier, farmers bred animals and crops to achieve desired characteristics. Although the genes were invisible, their influence in heredity was observable. James Watson and Francis Crick lifted the veil through which Mendel worked and revolutionized the understanding of genetics when they determined the double helix structure of DNA in the first half of the twentieth century. Subsequent research, especially through the multinational Human Genome Project (HGP), accelerated the understanding of the human genome and produced technologies that greatly increased the capacity for identifying associations of particular genes with particular physical conditions.

A. The Nature of Genetic Information

Molecular genetics and heredity are often viewed as coextensive, with the power of the more recently developed tools in genetic diagnosis simply enhancing information that lies below the surface of family medical history. For example, in a family with a *dominant monogenic* condition like the debilitating, lethal, late onset Huntington's Disease (HD), predictions based on its observed pattern of heredity would indicate that each child of a couple in which one parent has HD has a 50% chance of developing the disease. A genetic test, however, is able to tell each individual child if she herself has either a 100% or 0% chance of suffering the disease.

Thus, the newer form of genetic information carries an aura of certainty and determinism. Although in some cases, genetic information does have this power, this image is dangerously inaccurate in others. The vast majority of genetically linked medical conditions, in fact, do not fit the HD profile. Instead, for most of the genetic associations identified so far, the strongest conclusion that can be drawn is that this particular person *may* have a degree of escalated risk, often quite small, as compared to the general population. For *multifactorial* conditions, such as most genetically linked forms of cancer, particular genes contribute only a portion of the cause of the disease, and a person with the "gene for" that cancer has only an increased risk of the disease. Furthermore, even where some forms of a particular cancer have a genetic link, the vast majority of cases of the disease, including breast cancer, are entirely unrelated to heredity.

Molecular genetics is actually increasing uncertainty in some circumstances by revealing previously unknown manifestations of well-studied inherited conditions. For example, pedigree studies of families with members with cystic fibrosis (CF) showed the disease to be a *recessive monogenic* condition in which each child of a couple where one parent has the gene has a 25% chance of inheriting the pair of genes required for developing the disease itself. Molecular genetic studies of families with the CF gene, however, have revealed that CF can occur in nearly undetectable forms rather than producing the most familiar and tragic form of the disease that is fatal at a young age. The presence of the gene pair alone does not tell whether this fetus or child will develop the life-threatening or the mildest form of the disease. Thus, the predictive quality of genetic information can be quite tentative despite the mantle of certainty it carries.

Although colloquial references to "genetics" most often use the term as a synonym for heredity, this breeds misunderstanding. Some genetic conditions are the result of mutations that occur only after birth, and some diseases appear both in forms influenced by congenital genetics and in forms that appear to be random. On the other hand, attempts to distinguish genetics and heredity entirely, as do many current genetics statutes, draw an untenable line. See Section II.B, below.

Genetic testing unavoidably reveals information about persons who have not been tested. For example, if a genetic test shows that an individual has the HD gene, at least one of his parents also has the gene and will certainly develop the disease. They will learn this without being tested themselves and whether or not they would have chosen to know. Diagnostic genetic testing of a child or fetus may unexpectedly reveal that the man believing himself the father is not. Further, genetic testing for some conditions, such as for the mutations of BrCa1 associated with breast cancer, depends not only on the genetic test of a single individual but rather, require genetic testing of family members to realize the test's full predictive value.

B. Legal History of Genetics

In the most prominent judicial opinion on genetics, the Supreme Court decided that the forced sterilization of a woman believed to be intellectually impaired, whose mother and grandmother were also mistakenly believed to be mentally impaired, was justified by a legitimate state interest and did not violate the woman's constitutional rights. In Buck v. Bell, 274 U.S. 200, 47 S.Ct. 584, 71 L.Ed. 1000 (1927), Justice Oliver Wendell Holmes infamously declared in the Opinion of the Court: "Three generations of imbeciles are enough." The Supreme Court was not alone, however, in supporting legal enforcement of the principles of the eugenics movement that took hold in the U.S. in the 1920s.

Thirty states implemented programs that forcibly sterilized low-income, uneducated, or mentally impaired individuals as a selective population control program. More than 65,000 individuals nationwide were involuntarily sterilized in programs that extended through the mid 1970s. States also enacted legislation in the 1970s requiring that African–Americans be screened for the sickle-cell trait, despite the fact that individuals who had only one copy of the gene would suffer no physical effects and that there was no cure for the disease. The programs resulted in widespread confusion about sickle-cell trait and resulted in job and insurance discrimination. State-mandated genetic screening programs have expanded. See Section IV, below.

As with the regulation of research with human subjects discussed in Chapter 8, regulation of the use of genetic information is influenced by its history. In the case of genetics, the law partnered with often imperfect science to disadvantage particular groups. These concerns and experiences contributed to the adoption of current legal standards that treat genetic information specially.

II. DEFINITIONAL ISSUES

A. Genetics and Illness

Calling something a genetic anomaly, a genetic condition, a genetic defect, a genetic trait, or a genetic disease incorporates notions of health, illness, and normalcy in the human genotype (the genetic composition of a human being). Viewing a particular genetic trait as disease or abnormality stimulates claims that the trait should be corrected or fixed or avoided, with serious implications for respect for persons, equality, and payment for medical costs.

In Katskee v. Blue Cross/Blue Shield of Nebraska, 515 N.W.2d 645 (Neb. 1994), for example, the court held that the insurer must pay for a mastectomy and hysterectomy for a patient diagnosed with breast-ovarian carcinoma syndrome, which the insurer conceded was an accurate diagnosis based solely on family history. The court held that the insured was ill within the meaning of the term in the insurance policy, even though she did not have cancer, had no symptoms of dysfunction, and may never develop cancer. The same court, however, had held in an earlier case that a condition does not become an illness, and so is not a preexisting condition, until symptoms are manifest.

In addition, the emergence of genetic or genomic medicine, which employs genetic diagnosis and genetically targeted pharmaceuticals and biologics, is raising new standards of care for the practice of medicine. At the same time, the practice is raising issues of payment and equitable access to this level of care.

It may be difficult to distinguish between correcting a genetic defect and enhancing genetic traits that fall within the range of normal or average. This problem already confronts non-genetic medicine in the form of steroids for athletic performance, for example, or growth hormone to increase height. In fact, innumerable medical interventions could be considered either therapeutic or enhancing, depending on one's view of what is normal or natural and what is dysfunctional, with implications for payment. Treatment for genetic conditions raises a unique issue, however, as some interventions may alter genes for generations rather than just for the individual patient. Techniques, such as germ line as compared to somatic cell transfers, make the new traits inheritable. Selection of genetic traits in reproduction, through pre-implantation genetic diagnosis of embryos and prenatal genetic screening, are common, however, and may ultimately result in the drastic reduction of particular genetic conditions in the general population.

B. Statutory Definitions of Genetic Information

Many states and the federal government have enacted legislation to regulate the use of genetic information. These statutes vary significantly in their definition of genetic information, and that definition determines whether particular conditions fall within the nondiscrimination, confidentiality, and privacy protections afforded by the statute.

Some statutes, for example, apply only to laboratory tests of DNA, while others include family medical history within the definition of genetics. In the case of HD, discussed in Section I.A, above, only an individual who has been tested for the gene will come within the protection of a statute that defines genetic information as the results of a laboratory test of DNA, and an individual who has a family history of the disease but has not been tested would not. The federal Genetic Information Nondiscrimination Act (GINA) uses the broader definition and covers the results of the genetic tests of the individual, tests of his or her family members, and family medical history.

Most of these statutes distinguish between situations in which the genetically related illness has become manifest and those in which the individual remains asymptomatic for the disease. Generally, statutory restrictions are lifted when an illness has become symptomatic. See Section III.B.1, below.

Genetic discrimination statutes also may distinguish among different types of genetic illness. For example, some statutes cover only those illnesses which arise "solely" from an abnormality in the genes and exclude from their coverage those conditions, such as multifactorial genetic illnesses (See Section I.A, above), to which genes contribute only partly. Others include both types of genetically linked conditions—both those caused solely by a genetic trait and those in which a genetic trait is associated with increased risk.

III. LEGAL CLAIMS RELATING TO CONFIDENTIALITY, PRIVACY, AND DISCRIMINATION

A. Confidentiality and Privacy

1. Confidentiality

The issue of confidentiality of medical information involves both the duty to keep information confidential and the rare obligation to disclose information. Statutes and common law doctrines applying to medical information generally, such as the federal Health Insurance Portability and Accountability Act (HIPAA), apply to genetic information. In addition, many states have enacted genetics-specific confidentiality and privacy statutes.

The physician-patient relationship ordinarily includes a common law duty of confidentiality on the part of the doctor toward the patient. In unusual circumstances, however, the doctor may have the obligation or the authority to reveal otherwise confidential medical information under a common law "duty to warn." Statutes also may require disclosure, prohibit disclosure, or authorize disclosure at the doctor's discretion under particular circumstances.

Because of the implications of genetic information for family members, persons other than the patient may have a serious interest in genetic information, either because of their own risk of disease or because of decisions related to childbearing. In Safer v. Estate of Pack, 677 A.2d 1188 (N.J. App. 1996) and Pate v. Threlkel, 661 So.2d 278 (Fla. 1995), courts considered claims that doctors treating a patient for a genetically linked disease should have warned the patient or the family of the genetic basis of the disease and the risk of inheritability. The New Jersey appellate court in *Safer* held that the doctor had the duty to inform the patient's daughter; and the Florida Supreme Court in *Pate*, that the doctor had the duty to inform only the patient, and not other family members. A duty to warn, if recognized, would exist only where the risk of disease can be eliminated or mitigated.

HIPAA privacy regulations accommodate state law disclosure requirements. HIPAA regulations permit, but do not require, disclosure that the health care provider believes in good faith is required to prevent or lessen imminent threat.

Some state statutes address disclosure of genetic information in some detail and typically, restrictively. The New Jersey statute enacted after *Safer*, for example, permits only disclosures necessary for criminal proceedings; by order of a court; for the purpose of identifying bodies or for medical diagnosis of relatives of a decedent; and to the state's DNA database of convicted sex offenders. Disclosures of the sort required in *Safer* are not included among those permitted.

2. Privacy

Genetics privacy and confidentiality statutes also address genetics information held outside of the physician-patient relationship. Most, for example, prohibit health insurers from collecting genetic information, however it is defined in the statute, other than that necessary for treatment or payment. Prohibitions against collecting genetic information protect its privacy and are viewed as essential to the effectiveness of statutory prohibitions against discrimination on the basis of genetic characteristics. See Section III.B, below.

Privacy is also protected by statutory prohibitions against genetic testing without consent. Privacy concerns are raised in the collection and storage of genetic material in biobanks (see Section V.A, below) and in mandatory newborn genetic screening (see Section IV, below).

B. Discrimination

If a statute prohibits only decisions based on medical information produced by tests on DNA and not that derived from family medical history (see Section II.B., above), one may view this as an unjustified form of "genetic exceptionalism" in which the legislation gives a special privilege to one form of genetic information as compared to another. Some justify the special protection for genetic testing, however, as a necessary counterweight to widely held fears of discrimination in employment or health insurance that may lead individuals to avoid genetic testing. Moreover, even the broader definition of genetic information is subject to the charge of genetic exceptionalism, as statutes covering both genetic testing and family medical history treat genetically related illness preferentially as compared to other health status issues.

1. Discrimination in Insurance

State statutes prohibiting genetic discrimination in insurance generally distinguish among different forms of insurance. For example, it is quite common for legislation to prohibit discrimination in health insurance but to exclude life insurance, credit insurance, or other insurance policies. Most statutes prohibiting the use of genetic information in health insurance provide that the insurer may not refuse to issue a policy and may not use such information in setting premiums or benefits.

The statutes allow insurers to take into account genetically linked illnesses that have become symptomatic. Allowing insurers to refuse to insure or to exclude preexisting conditions in persons who already have symptomatic disease avoids adverse selection where individuals choose to purchase insurance only when they have been diagnosed with an active illness.

2.   Discrimination in Employment

Some states have enacted legislation prohibiting the use of genetic information in employment. The federal GINA also prohibits employers from using genetic information in hiring, discharge, compensation, and other employment decisions. The federal Americans with Disabilities Act (ADA) continues to apply to employers for adverse employment decisions based on a person's medical condition when that condition amounts to a disability, as defined by the Act.

GINA protects an individual only where the genetically linked illness is asymptomatic, and the ADA protects an individual only where the genetically linked illness has already developed and so impairs the individual as to constitute a disability (or produces impairments that are viewed as disabilities). An individual who has a genetically linked illness that is less than debilitating is not protected by either statute, unless he can come within the ADA's provision for those "viewed as" having a disability.

GINA also limits employers in collecting genetic information on applicants and employees, but with several exceptions. These exceptions account for employers who provide health services to employees and for genetic monitoring of employees for workplace safety, provided the monitoring program meets particular standards.

The ADA also governs the employer's collection of medical information, including genetic information, from employees. In 2002, Burlington Northern Santa Fe Railway (BNSF) agreed to pay 36 workers $2.2 million to settle litigation brought under the ADA. BNSF had tested workers who filed claims for workers' compensation for carpal tunnel syndrome without the workers' knowledge or consent. See also, Norman–Bloodsaw v. Lawrence Berkeley Laboratory, 135 F.3d 1260 (9th Cir. 1998), rejecting defendant's motion to dismiss plaintiffs' claims under Title VII and Constitutional privacy protections for employer's testing for sickle-cell trait without the knowledge and consent of employees.

IV. MANDATORY NEWBORN GENETIC SCREENING

A. Background

State mandated newborn genetic screening began in the 1960s with screening for PKU, a congenital disease that leads to mental retardation or death if left untreated. The condition occurs in 1/10,000–1/15,000 births. The treatment involves a restricted diet that must be followed from birth to avoid the disease's effects. PKU screening is commonly viewed as a success story because the disease can be easily treated and serious injuries thereby avoided. Critics point out, however, that the test has a significant false positive rate; that the diet can itself cause brain damage and death in infants without the disease; that there was no evidence that pediatricians would not have routinely offered the test without legal mandate; and that the owner of the test was the primary advocate for its adoption by the states.

With the perceived success of PKU screening and the development of new technologies that test for large numbers of genetic traits with the same blood sample and very low marginal costs, states have greatly expanded their mandatory newborn genetic screening programs. State programs now test for as few as seven or as many as seventy-five genetic conditions. The federal Newborn Screening Saves Lives Act of 2007 provides federal support for expanding these programs.

B.   State Authority

Under the police power, the states have the authority to advance the health and welfare of their citizens. Where screening detects genetic traits related to treatable disease, the justification of state mandate is avoidance of disease. Some argue, however, that the police power does not extend to medical conditions that are not infectious or to screening for genetic traits that produce conditions that are not treatable.

The state may also claim that it is acting *in parens patriae* to protect children through newborn genetic screening. Exercise of state control over medical decision making for children, however, usually requires a finding of neglect to displace the parent's authority with that of the state.

C. Parental Consent

Most of the state statutes requiring consent for genetic testing generally include newborn screening among those exceptions in which consent is not required. A significant number of states allow parents to opt out of testing for their child only if they have a religious objection. Only a small number of states require parental consent or allow parents to opt out for other than religious reasons. In Douglas County v. Anaya, 694 N.W.2d 601 (Neb. 2005), the court upheld mandatory screening over the parents' objection against Constitutional challenge, a case later used by state officials to seize an infant from the same family for legally required testing.

D. Benefits and Risks

PKU screening produces benefits to infants in whom the condition is detected because the prescribed diet prevents serious injury. Where there is no treatment available, or where treatment is available but not accessible either because of geographic or financial constraints on the family, the significant benefit of the PKU screening model is not present. For conditions without treatment, the benefit (or burden) of screening is the family's knowing of the child's disease-related genetic trait and the opportunity that may exist for subsequent reproductive decision making.

The balance of benefits and risks is significantly influenced by the accuracy of the test and the quality of its administration as both false negatives and false positives present risks. False negatives provide false assurances of the absence of particular genes and may delay accurate diagnosis. False positives trigger unnecessary treatment that may harm healthy infants. Even accurate positive results produce some risks, including the risks of treatment as well as burdens associated with viewing one's child or oneself as ill, particularly in the case of adult-onset genetic illnesses.

E. Retention of Samples

The blood spot cards used for newborn screening typically are held by the state indefinitely. See Section V.A, below. While many states address the retention of genetic samples generally, few specifically reference the samples taken in newborn screening. These samples become a "biobank" or a "DNA database" that can provide raw material for forensic identification and for research. In addition, the screening program itself may be engaged in research on the validity of the tests themselves.

V. GENETIC RESEARCH

Genetic research involves both research to identify the associations between genes and diseases or other conditions and clinical research investigating the use of genetic diagnosis and genetic therapies. Federal and state regulations that apply to research generally apply also to genetic research. See Chapter 8. This section addresses only those issues that are particular to genetic research.

A. Biobanks

A significant number of private and public-private ventures are responding to increasing demand for raw material for genetic research. These ventures combine large collections of tissue, medical records, disease registries, blood spots, and other information that are already collected and maintained by health care providers, academic research organizations, and state and federal governments and make them available to researchers.

1. Consent

Federal regulations govern consensual and non-consensual use of medical information and physical specimens in research. Current federal standards require consent for the collection of specimens and personal information but allow nonconsensual use of stored tissue and information, provided the material is made unidentifiable for the research process. See Section IV.A in Chapter 8. Genetic confidentiality or nondiscrimination statutes in some states add requirements beyond those in the federal regulations, including specific provisions relating to consent for use of genetic information in research.

2. Risk–Benefit Analysis

Regulations governing research with human subjects in the U.S. require institutional review boards (IRBs) to consider the balance of risk and benefit in each research protocol. See Section IV.A in Chapter 8. The IRB is to consider all forms of risk to the subject, including psychological, social, and legal risks as well as physical risks of pain and injury.

The individual subject may suffer psychological harm as a result of diagnosis of presymptomatic conditions that were unknown to the subject. Social harm may occur in studies where the results stigmatize particular population subgroups by associating them with disease and disability. Managing the risk of social harm is complicated by the fact that the individuals consenting to the research are, in effect, acting on behalf of an entire population. Special privacy and confidentiality concerns also arise in genetics research because of the information that the specimens and medical records carry about nonparticipating and nonconsenting family members. See Section I.A, above.

3.　Property Claims

Property claims to the products of research are asserted among researchers and between researchers and research subjects. The products of research generally are protected by patent law as intellectual property. The application of patent law to genetics has been controversial as a matter of the application of patent law to this type of material and for its impact on medical research and treatment. Patents are not available for natural objects, but patents have been available for decades for genetically engineered bacteria and are available for genetic sequences as well. The patenting of DNA sequences, and particularly fragments of sequences, has raised considerable concerns when patent owners have refused to release the sequences to the research community or have used them to discourage the development or use of diagnostic or therapeutic tools. If an entity holds the patent on a particular sequence (such as the BrCa1 gene associated with some inheritable forms of breast cancer, for example), that firm can exclude others from using the test for the gene for research, diagnosis, or treatment or can charge substantial licensing fees.

Some have argued that DNA sequences should be considered a commons, available to all for the development of lifesaving medical interventions, while others argue that the property rights recognized by a patent are necessary to encourage capable research entities to invest in genetic research. Technology used to isolate genetic sequences has been funded substantially by federal funds through the Human Genome Project. Some argue, therefore, that granting patents on DNA sequences allows some to take advantage of public funding for private gain. Federal law, however, has encouraged private ownership of the results of federally funded research for some time. See Section V.B.1 in Chapter 8.

The courts thus far have been less hospitable to property claims asserted by the research subjects to the profits or control of the products. To the extent that a limited property right is acknowledged, the courts have thus far treated those rights as seriously limited in character or extinguished by the patient's or research participant's donation or relinquishment of the genetic material or genetic information. See Section V.B.2 in Chapter 8.

B. Clinical Genetic Research

Clinical genetic research is governed by the federal regulations applicable to any research with human subjects and by a special regime for research involving the introduction of recombinant DNA into human cells, as is done in gene therapy. Under FDA regulations, such research must be approved by the research organization's institutional review board and then must be reviewed and approved by a special committee of the FDA, after public notice. See discussion of IRBs and research review process in Chapter 8.

FDA review focuses on the traditional concerns of research with human subjects, but adds consideration of ethical and social implications specific to genetic research. In particular, there is a concern that the therapy not affect the reproductive cells of the subject and that commercial interests in the research (such as an interest in patenting the products) not interfere with communication of results among researchers and to the public.

Clinical genetic research produced one of the most infamous recent cases concerning the participation of human beings as subjects in research. Jesse Gelsinger, a young man with a genetic liver disease, died as a result of an experiment with gene therapy. Subsequent investigation of the behavior of the researcher and the research organization revealed the financial interests of each that may have influenced the approval and the conduct of the protocol and highlighted commercial interests in research generally. See Section V.B.1 in Chapter 8.

CHAPTER 4

LEGAL STANDARDS FOR THE DETERMINATION OF DEATH

I. INTRODUCTION

Determining the exact point at which death occurs can be legally significant. The law of estates, for example, uses the time of death to determine the precedence of interrelated wills, and a charge of homicide typically requires that death have occurred within one year of assault.

A clear determination of the point of death is critical for medical decision making. In the case of retrieval of organs for transplantation, for example, the donor must be dead before life-sustaining organs are removed and time is critical, as discussed in Chapter 7. For a patient who is living, the decision to continue or withdraw medical care follows the framework described in Chapter 5 and generally focuses on the individual patient's own values and choices. Once the person is dead under applicable legal standards, however, the duty to provide medical treatment for that person ceases.

For centuries, the common law standard of death held that death occurred when the individual's heart and lung functions ceased. The irreversible cessation of cardio-pulmonary function was observable to anyone, and no effective interventions existed to restart these functions once they had stopped.

The development of effective resuscitation interventions presented the question of irreversibility of the cessation of cardiopulmonary function. In addition, the medical capacity to mechanically maintain heart and lung functions over ever longer periods of time separated cardiopulmonary function from brain function. It was possible for the ventilator (and associated medical interventions) to maintain the cardiopulmonary function in an individual whose brain had completely and irretrievably ceased to function.

II. CURRENT LEGAL STANDARDS

In 1968, an interdisciplinary work group at Harvard published a report stating their consensus that irreversible cessation of all brain function, now called brain death, should be accepted as the point at which death should be declared. The Harvard Committee believed that this "whole brain" death standard would accomplish two goals. First, the Committee believed that families should not be asked to make the decision to remove ventilator support from such an individual, and that physicians alone should make that decision. The report was published years before it was clear that the law would support the removal of ventilator support from any patient at all. Second, the Committee understood that the total brain death standard would permit the retrieval of vital organs for transplantation, avoiding the inevitable physical decay that occurs during ventilator support of an individual with no brain function.

Even though the authors of the report, including the lawyer member of the group, stated that no change in the law was necessary, their work eventually led to legislation nearly immediately in a few states and to the development of several model statutes proposed by scholars and professional organizations including the ABA and the AMA.

Eventually, the Uniform Determination of Death Act of 1980 (UDDA) adopted the whole brain death standard. The UDDA provides that an individual is dead if *either* cardiopulmonary function *or* "all functions of the entire brain, including the brain stem" have irreversibly ceased. All states now have adopted the total brain death standard of the UDDA by statute, regulation, or case law; however, the actual language of the state statutes varies considerably. These variations could be significant, but have not yet had a substantial practical legal effect. This Section refers primarily to the UDDA.

A. Irreversible Cessation of Cardiopulmonary Function

The UDDA does not abandon the cardiopulmonary measure of death. Rather, it offers the irreversible cessation of cardiopulmonary function and total brain function as alternative indicators of death. In most circumstances, death is still determined with the cardiopulmonary standard; only rarely, is there any direct measurement of brain function, typically when cardiopulmonary function is being maintained mechanically.

The UDDA makes it clear that an individual whose heart has stopped is not dead unless the condition is irreversible. The requirement that the cessation of cardiopulmonary function be irreversible raises some practical concerns. First, people commonly, and mistakenly, say that they "died" if their heart has stopped even though they were resuscitated and so their condition did not meet the legal standard of death. Second, and more importantly, determination of irreversibility is a matter of judgment in particular cases.

The UDDA does not itself require an effort at resuscitation to determine whether the cessation of cardiopulmonary function is irreversible. A physician may decide that resuscitation will be ineffective, concluding that the condition is irreversible, and declare the patient to be dead. Or, resuscitation may be forgone for other reasons, and eventually it is impossible to restore function. See Section D, below, and Chapter 5.

B. Functions of the Entire Brain

Mechanically maintaining heart and lung function preserves the appearance of life even if the brain has no activity whatsoever: blood circulates, body temperature remains warm, other organs such as kidneys and liver continue to function, and mechanical ventilation inflates and deflates the lungs. For this reason, the determination of death by the irreversible cessation of total brain function is sometimes called "brain death" as if the patient is not completely dead. Although according to law, the individual is dead, news articles and health professionals frequently refer to a "brain dead" individual being kept "alive," for example to extend a pregnancy.

The UDDA and all current state laws require the irreversible cessation of all brain function, including the brain stem, if death is to be declared based on the brain function criterion. This requirement distinguishes the brain death situation from others in which the patient has some even minimal brain function and would not be considered dead. See Section III, below. Although the whole brain death standard is very well accepted in law, there is still some discomfort and skepticism about brain death in both directions, with some philosophers and physicians arguing that it is too narrow and should be expanded and others arguing that the brain death standard embeds particular values that are not universally shared. See Sections III and II.C, below.

C. Accommodation of Individual Beliefs

Hospitals sometimes encounter surviving family members who reject the application of the whole brain death standard for their kin. Although the law is clear that doctors and hospitals have the legal authority to declare the individual dead without the consent of the family, some hospitals routinely respond to the family's concern at least temporarily by delaying the declaration of death for some time. Ultimately, however, most hospitals will discontinue ventilator support in these cases over the family's objection.

At least two states, however, have established legal rights for individuals who reject the brain death standard. New Jersey by statute provides that the neurological criteria should not be used to determine death where the doctor "has reason to believe" that the use of the brain death criteria would violate the patient's "personal religious beliefs." New York State Department of Health regulations require that hospitals provide reasonable accommodation for those with "religious or moral objections" to the use of the neurological criteria for death. The regulations specify, however, that the hospitals need not accommodate objections based "solely on the psychological denial that death has occurred or on an alleged inadequacy of the brain death determination."

D. Organ Donation After Circulatory Determination of Death

Organ donation after circulatory determination of death (DCDD, also called non-heart-beating donors, donation after cardiopulmonary or cardiac death, donors without heartbeat, and asystolic donors) relies on the cardiopulmonary arm of the UDDA. DCDD occurs in two circumstances—controlled DCDD and uncontrolled or unanticipated DCDD. In controlled DCDD, the patient is dependent on life-sustaining treatment (most typically, a ventilator) and has decided, either by his own choice or by proxy, to terminate the life supportive treatment and donate his organs. Life support is removed in the operating room; the physician waits a specified amount of time; death is declared; and the organs are removed. In uncontrolled or unanticipated DCDD, an individual experiences an unexpected cardiac arrest due to traumatic injury or disease. The individual may arrive dead on arrival at the hospital or may not respond to resuscitation. Controlled DCDD is the more common scenario of the two.

DCDD is controversial for several reasons. Opponents argue that the current practice assures neither that the heartbeat cannot resume nor that the patient's brain has ceased functioning at the time the organs are removed. They argue that while the UDDA does not require measurement of brain function, the Act uses a unitary determination of death: the cessation of cardiopulmonary function and the cessation of brain function are merely two ways to measure that a person is dead and not two forms of death. Proponents argue that neither determination of brain function nor resuscitation efforts are required under the law; in fact, that resuscitative efforts are prohibited if the patient has refused them; and that the wait between cessation of cardiac function and removal of the organs (often including the heart) assures that cardiac function will not resume spontaneously. Proponents of DCDD accept that some brain function may continue for up to fifteen minutes after the heart stops beating but that brain death is not legally, or philosophically, required.

The claim for longer wait times is quite significant for the recovery of organs for transplantation as the longer the wait the less viable the organ. Wait times vary considerably in practice and generally range from two to five minutes. Of course, the variations in wait time raise some liability risks for DCDD.

A second issue in DCDD is that that the patient will be subject to some medical interventions—to thin the blood, reduce body temperature, expand the blood vessels—prior to termination of life sustaining treatment to improve the condition of the organs and the ultimate success of their transplantation. In some cases, the patient will have specifically consented to these procedures, but in others the patient may not have anticipated them when he executed an advance directive to terminate treatment or to donate organs upon death. The advance directive and the document of gift for organ donation may actually conflict, with the one directing that medical interventions be discontinued and the other giving permission for the procedures necessary for retrieval and donation. States are beginning to address the issue of consent and conflicting advance directives, and some statutes specifically authorize interventions to preserve the organs until apparent conflicts can be resolved.

There has been some concern expressed as well that interventions to preserve the health of the organs may hasten the death of the donors. Some individual health care providers may object to participating in DCDD, and so claims of protection for conscience may arise. See Section IV.B in Chapter 1. Despite the ambiguity in the application of the legal standard for the determination of death and ethical concerns with DCDD, it has become a common practice.

III. PROPOSALS FOR EXPANDING STANDARDS FOR THE DETER- MINATION OF DEATH

A. "Higher" Brain Death

Some argue that cessation of brain activity in the higher or upper brain alone should be recognized as the state of death. In such a condition, the individual would have a functioning brain stem that would maintain the most basic physical functions, but would lack consciousness and any ability to perceive or communicate. Claims that permanent and irreversible unconsciousness should be recognized as death rely on a consciousness-centered measure of personhood. Opponents argue that calling persons, such as those in the persistent vegetative state, dead makes distinctions between such a condition and other states of unconsciousness or brain damage illusory. Proponents argue that the whole brain death standard itself requires some line-drawing regarding what counts as brain activity to address problems such as isolated cellular activity.

Proposals to expand the standard for determining death to include higher brain death have not been successful. While persons in such states are not declared dead, however, life-sustaining treatment may be terminated. See Chapter 5. In some cases of termination of life-sustaining treatment, organs will be retrieved using DCDD. See Section II.D, above.

B.　Brain Absence

An infant born with anencephaly is born without any upper brain at all and with a large cavity where the back of the skull ordinarily would be. The child has a functioning brain stem, however, which maintains the basic physical functions, just as it does in the case of PVS. See Section III.A, above.

For a period of time in the early 1990s, some momentum developed for either extending the neurological criteria for death to include the condition of "brain absence" or allowing life-sustaining organs to be removed from anencephalic infants in a singular exception to the "dead donor" rule. See Section II.E in Chapter 7. In 1992, the Florida Supreme Court refused to extend the legal standard for the determination of death to include anencephaly and rejected the parents' claim that they be able to donate the organs for transplantation. In re T.A.C.P., 609 So.2d 588 (Fla. 1992). "Brain absence'' was not accepted as a legal standard for the determination of death, although the court noted that under the common law and the Florida statute, the court had the authority to do so.

CHAPTER 5

DECISIONS REGARDING LIFE–SUSTAINING TREATMENT

I. THE U.S. CONSTITUTION AND THE "RIGHT TO DIE:" THE *CRUZAN* CASE

In Cruzan v. Director, Missouri Department of Health, 497 U.S. 261, 110 S.Ct. 2841, 111 L.Ed.2d 224 (1990), the Supreme Court considered its first case on the withholding or withdrawing life-sustaining medical care. For over a decade prior to *Cruzan*, state courts had been deciding similar cases relying on the law applicable to guardianships for incompetent patients and tort law regarding informed consent and battery for medical treatment to which the patient had not consented. Some earlier state courts had also relied on the U.S. constitution, primarily the right to privacy found in the Fourteenth Amendment that protected the individual's right to make certain health care decisions (for example, as to contraception and abortion) free from governmental prohibition. Nearly every case had decided that life-sustaining treatment could be withdrawn.

Nancy Cruzan's parents had decided to discontinue medically provided nutrition and hydration for their adult daughter who had been unconscious in a persistent vegetative state for seven years and who was cared for in a state-owned and operated facility. The State of Missouri refused to comply with the parents' request, and the Missouri Supreme Court (in a 4–3 decision) held that the parents lacked the necessary "clear and convincing evidence" that their daughter would have wanted to have that treatment stopped.

Chief Justice Rehnquist wrote the opinion of the Court in *Cruzan*, with four Justices dissenting and two Justices concurring in the result but for entirely inconsistent reasons. The Court's opinion lacks any strong and unqualified statement concerning the existence or scope of relevant Constitutional rights because of its need to retain the two concurring Justices for a majority, and, perhaps, because the Court anticipated later claims of Constitutional protection for physician-assisted death. Ultimately, the Court held that Missouri was permitted to apply its clear and convincing evidence standard when determining whether there was sufficient evidence to justify the removal of life-sustaining medical treatment from an incompetent person. The Court did not even mention the term "privacy," which had created such division in the abortion cases, preferring instead to ask whether the application of the Missouri standard of proof intruded upon a "liberty interest" protected by the Fourteenth Amendment.

The Court's opinion first addressed the rights of *competent* patients, saying that "a constitutionally protected liberty interest in refusing unwanted medical treatment may be inferred from our prior decisions." The opinion then went on to describe concerns over whether decisions on behalf of incompetent persons are qualitatively the same as decisions made by the competent patient for himself, although it did not resolve that issue. Further, without delineating the content of any supposed Constitutional right, the Court's opinion noted that "it cannot be disputed that the Due Process clause protects an interest in life as well as an interest in refusing life-sustaining treatment."

The Court's opinion did not distinguish between medically provided nutrition and hydration and other life-sustaining treatment. The opinion states that it assumes "for purposes of this case" that the Constitution "would grant a competent person a constitutionally protected right to refuse lifesaving nutrition and hydration," again restricting its statement to the competent patient rather than to Nancy Cruzan's particular situation. The opinion further notes that the State may intervene when a "physically-able adult" decides "to starve to death."

In the end, Justice Rehnquist's opinion addressed only a narrow question: whether the U.S. Constitution prohibited the State of Missouri from choosing the "procedural requirement" that it did. The Court held that Missouri's rule applying a strict clear and convincing evidence standard advanced legitimate state interests in the preservation of human life and, more particularly, in assuring that the now-incompetent individual's choices are accurately understood. Although the Court did not go so far as to say a state would be required to do so, the Court announced that a state could choose to apply an evidentiary standard in these cases that would err on the side of preserving life.

The four dissenters, none of whom are still on the Court, all argued that the Constitution provides a right for patients and their surrogates to refuse life-sustaining treatment without substantial interference from the state. They each argued that Missouri's rule created an insurmountable barrier to proper surrogate decision making. As it turned out, after the Supreme Court's decision the trial judge considered newly discovered evidence of conversations that Ms. Cruzan had some years earlier with friends and determined that there was clear and convincing evidence that she would want life-sustaining treatment to be withdrawn.

Justice O'Connor and Justice Scalia wrote the two concurring opinions. Justice O'Connor asserted that there is a Constitutional right to refuse treatment, including nutrition and hydration. Further, although she was willing to accept the narrow holding in this particular case, her opinion noted that decisions made by a patient-appointed surrogate would be Constitutionally protected against state interference. In contrast, Justice Scalia argued that "federal courts have no business in this field" and that the withdrawal of nutrition and hydration should be considered suicide and left entirely to state regulation.

Cruzan had little effect on case law concerning refusal of life-sustaining treatment. The case stimulated state legislation, however, to expand the scope of advance directives and surrogate decision making. See Section IV.B, below.

II. COMPETENT PATIENTS

A. The General Rule: The Patient Decides

The basic rule of health care decision making is that a competent patient may make his own healthcare decisions. The common law basis of this principle is generally traced back to Judge Cardozo's opinion in Schloendorff v. Society of New York Hospital, 211 N.Y. 125, 105 N.E. 92 (N.Y.1914), a medical battery case in which that court determined that, "Every human being of adult years and sound mind has a right to determine what shall be done with his own body...." That principle has since been explicated and limited by courts in virtually every state, but it still provides the starting point for an analysis of a patient's right to forgo even life-sustaining medical treatment. The American Medical Association has confirmed the general ethical principle that a competent patient can choose to withhold or withdraw life prolonging medical treatment (in the words of the AMA's Council on Ethical and Judicial Affairs), and this ethical determination has strengthened the American courts' willingness to recognize patient authority to make these decisions.

As a general matter, courts have extended this principle to both terminally ill patients and patients who have determined that their quality of life makes their life not worth sustaining, even when they are not terminally ill. Thus, courts have found that competent patients may choose to forgo treatment (like ventilator therapy and tube feeding) for chronic conditions even though they could live for years if they were provided the proposed treatment. In doing so, courts argue that they are vindicating the patients' interest in maintaining dignity and quality of life, and, in the words of one California court, avoiding "ignominy, embarrassment, humiliation and dehumanizing" aspects of any underlying condition. Some see the court's use of these words as evidence of the dangerous disrespect our society maintains for the severely ill who decide to continue their lives despite their illnesses.

The motives of a patient in discontinuing care are irrelevant, as long as the patient is competent. Thus, the fact that a patient's choice is based on religious principles most people would consider irrational is legally meaningless. A competent adult Jehovah's Witness may refuse a blood transfusion and a competent adult Christian Scientist may turn down all medical care. Of course, if that refusal results, down the road, in the patient losing the competency to make health care decisions, a new decision making principle will then have to be put in place.

B. Countervailing State Interests

There are limitations on a patient's right to make health care decisions, though. For almost half a century American courts have repeated, almost as a mantra, the four countervailing state interests that may limit competent (and incompetent) patients' right to determine their own care: (1) the preservation of life, (2) the protection of innocent third parties, (3) the prevention of suicide, and (4) the maintenance of the ethical integrity of the medical profession. All four countervailing interests have been heavily criticized, and each has been formally rejected by some courts. Still, they provide the starting point for analysis of whether the general rule will be applied. If none of these four countervailing interests is sufficient, the patient's decision prevails.

1. Preservation of Life

While a state may declare that it has a policy to preserve all life, as Missouri did in the *Cruzan* case, such a generalized policy is no longer sufficient to overcome the basic principle that a competent patient may refuse any treatment whatsoever. The nature of the state's interest in the preservation of life was the only countervailing state interest raised by the state in the *Cruzan* case, which, of course, did not involve a competent patient. The Chief Justice said that "a state may properly decline to make judgments about the 'quality' of life that a particular individual may enjoy, and simply assert an unqualified interest in the preservation of human life to be weighed against the constitutionally protected interests of the individual." Not surprisingly, the dissenters viewed the state's interest in the preservation of life very differently. Justice Stevens objected to Missouri's policy of "equating [Cruzan's] life with the biological persistence of her bodily functions." He pointed out that, "[l]ife, particularly human life, is not commonly thought of as a merely physiological condition or function. Its sanctity is often thought to derive from the impossibility of any such reduction. When people speak of life, they often mean to describe the experiences that comprise a person's history . . . ."

Justice Brennan was especially offended by the notion that the generalized state interest in life could overcome the liberty interest of a particular patient to forgo a particular life-sustaining treatment. One person's fundamental rights, he argued, may not be sacrificed for the abstract benefit of society. Thus, while a state may wish to demonstrate its respect for all life and avoid the erosion of this principle, courts are not likely to find that allowing competent patients to forgo treatment would result in the denigration of the value of life.

2. Protection of Innocent Third Parties

The protection of innocent third parties rarely arises in a right-to-die case involving a competent patient. When it does, though, some courts may be willing to seriously consider whether it is sufficient to overcome the general principle supporting a competent patient's right to choose to forgo treatment.

For example, if a patient's children will become orphaned as a result of the patient's choice to forgo simple and safe treatment like a blood transfusion, some judges are willing to find that there is a countervailing state interest in protecting the children that is sufficiently strong to overcome the general principle that the patient makes all health care decisions. This countervailing state interest in protecting children from becoming orphans, which is more concrete, secular and utilitarian than other countervailing interests, has been more important than the other countervailing interests in actual litigation, at least over the last decade, although even this reason has rarely been enough to limit a competent adult from making a health care decision.

3. Prevention of Suicide

The countervailing state interest in the prevention of suicide is really derivative of the interest in preserving life. Although the Supreme Court has confirmed that a state *could* make assisting suicide a crime, committing suicide is no longer a crime in any state. While there are powerful arguments that suicide creates serious problems for those who are left behind and thus should be subject to state regulation, the reasons that our society wants to discourage teen suicides from taking their own lives simply do not apply to cases where the suicide "victims" are terminally ill, in intractable suffering and in the midst of the dying process anyway. The real reason for the assertion of this state interest in the prevention of suicide in health care decision making cases was articulated by a dissenting judge in a Massachusetts right to die case: "suicide is direct self-destruction and is intrinsically evil. No set of circumstances can make it moral . . . ."

4. Maintenance of the Ethical Integrity of the Medical Profession

There is no longer any reason to believe that the ethics of the medical profession absolutely forbid discontinuation of medical treatment for a competent patient who chooses to reject that treatment. The American Medical Association has explicitly rejected that position, and other medical groups have taken a wide range of positions, with some articulating the importance of maintaining life under all circumstances, and others, at the other end of the spectrum, supporting direct physician action to affirmatively cause a patient's death under some circumstances. Even if there were a determinable ethical position of the medical profession, there is a question of whether the "ethical integrity of the medical profession" should ever overcome a patient's otherwise proper decision to forgo some form of treatment. It does not seem likely that this countervailing interest will be relevant to analyzing a competent patient's choice very often. In fact, it is increasingly clear that no countervailing state interest is likely to overcome a competent patient's choice under normal circumstances.

5.　Special Circumstances

There are a few special circumstances in which the interests of a competent patient are given less weight, or the interests of the state are considered especially important. For example, the national interest allows the military to require its soldiers to undergo life saving (or other) medical care so that they can be returned to the front, and a prisoner cannot condition accepting treatment that is necessary to save his life on concessions about the terms of his incarceration because the state's interest in "orderly prison administration" outweighs the right of the prisoner to refuse treatment. These kinds of limitations on the general principle are extremely rare.

III.　DETERMINING COMPETENCY

A.　Generally

If some decision making rights are available only to competent adults, the law must determine what constitutes competency for purposes of health care decisions. The requirement that decisions be made by competent adults grows out of the law of informed consent, which requires that consent be voluntary, informed, and competent. There are few detailed statutory definitions of competency, and the statutory treatment of this issue has been to focus on the process by which competency is determined rather than the substantive standards for finding competency. In fact, this is one of the rare areas of principle in which law declares the question to be a medical question, but medicine declares the question to be one of law. In the end, generally the law requires health care workers, often doctors, to testify as to incompetence (or even to declare incompetence) based on unarticulated legal and medical standards.

Over the past two decades new statutes and common law decisions touching on this issue have tended to use the term "decisional capacity" instead of competency, and a patient without competency to make a health care decision is said to lack "decisional capacity" to make that decision. The change in terminology is the result of legal efforts to indicate that competency, which had been used to identify a person as maintaining or lacking the ability to make a wide range of decisions, really had to be evaluated on a task-by-task and moment-by-moment basis. Thus, where patients used to be competent or incompetent, both law and medicine now recognize that a patient can have the capacity to make some decisions (to have a finger pricked for a blood test, for example) but not other decisions (to forgo life sustaining treatment or to undergo transplant surgery, for example). In addition, the use of the term "decisional capacity" reminds us that a patient could have capacity to make a decision upon awakening in the morning, but not just after (or just before) taking certain medications in the afternoon. Thus, a patient with variable capacity may have decision making capacity that varies depending on time, place, family support present at the moment, or nature of the decision to be made. Today both the term "decisional capacity" and the term "competency" are used to describe a patient quality that may be variable in all of these different ways.

A patient is presumed to have competency to make all health care decisions at all times and under all circumstances unless a formal determination is made that the patient lacks that capacity with regard to a certain kind of decision. Sometimes a patient's incompetency is obvious. There is no doubt that an unconscious patient is also an incompetent patient, at least during the period of his lack of consciousness. When the incompetency is not obvious, the law (or, in some jurisdictions, the medical custom, which has never been formally adopted by the law) requires a physician, usually a treating or supervising physician, to make a declaration of incompetency. In some states, more than one health care provider must conclude that a patient lacks competency, and in some states a patient with a particular condition—mental illness, for example— must be evaluated by at least one health care provider with experience working with patients with that condition. Either the law or customary medical practice requires that any nonobvious determination of incompetency be marked in the patient's chart. If the patient or anyone else objects to a finding of incompetency, the issue will be resolved judicially. In an overabundance of caution, health care providers may choose to seek an initial judicial determination of the patient's incompetency rather than make that decision themselves, although either procedural option (a declaration by a court, or a declaration by a provider, outside of the legal process but still subject to judicial review) is generally legally sufficient to allow the provider to treat the patient as someone who is incompetent.

B. President's Commission Standards

The underlying purpose of the rule that treats competent patients differently from patients who lack capacity is to serve the principle of autonomy by making sure that the values and interests of patients are honored in the decision making process. As the President's Commission for the Study of Ethical Problems in Medicine and Biomedical and Behavioral Research indicated three decades ago, the purpose of autonomy is served (and thus decision making capacity should exist) only when a patient "(1) possess[es] a set of values and goals; (2) [has] the ability to communicate and to understand information; and (3) [has] the ability to deliberate and reason about [the patient's] choice." Of course, it is not so easy to test a patient for these three attributes, all of which can be variable. There is no simple litmus test for capacity.

The evaluation of the first of these attributes— the possession of a set of values—maybe the hardest to translate into practical terms. The goal is to determine whether a patient is carrying out consistent values that the patient has demonstrated throughout life when the patient makes a health care decision. Of course, patients' values may change over a lifetime, or even all of a sudden, and facing death is exactly the kind of event that does change one's values. Thus, it makes sense to err on the side of finding that a patient's decision is based in a set of values that are consistently important to the patient unless it is very clear that it is not.

More commonly, a determination that a patient lacks competency is based either on the finding that a patient lacks the ability to communicate and understand information, or the finding that the patient is without ability to rationally evaluate the decision to be made. A patient who cannot communicate in any way—a patient who is unconscious, for example—clearly cannot meet the President's Commission's standards. Probably the most common basis for making determinations of incompetency is the finding that the patient is not capable of acting rationally. Note, though, that the President's Commission would not find a patient to lack decisional capacity just because that person is not acting logically; rather, it requires that the patient be *incapable* of deliberating and reasoning about the health care decision. A principle that would allow a physician to declare a patient incompetent because that patient is not acting rationally in making a particular decision would effectively allow the physician to substitute her view for that of the patient. The patient must be incapable of logic, not just fail to use logic in making a particular decision.

The problems inherent in determining a patient's competency makes it very easy to use this doctrine, developed to protect autonomy, to undermine that patient's autonomy. In fact, one of the best predictors that a physician will find a patient to be incompetent is the fact that the doctor would make a different decision than the one made by the patient. The predictive value of this factor goes up as the underlying health care decision becomes more important. This problem is exacerbated by the providers' tendency to have greater respect for the decisions of people who are like the provider. Well educated and wealthier patients sometimes may be found to have decisional capacity when similar patients without that background, and without families comfortable defending their relatives' competence, would be found incompetent. In addition, health care providers may factor a patient's depression into the competency calculus in different ways. While depression may make it difficult for a patient to exercise reason, in some cases a terminally ill patient's depression may be a sign of competence, not incompetence. After all, depression is one common reaction to facing an early death, and the patient who does not get depressed following a diagnosis that she is terminally ill is more likely to be the one who cannot think rationally than the one who is depressed by the prospect of imminent death.

There is a risk that doctors will try to save patients from making decisions they would not make themselves by finding those patients to lack decisional capacity. While, in theory, a patient who is competent to consent to life sustaining care is equally legally competent to deny consent, there are undoubtedly many cases in which a patient who would be permitted to consent to a particular treatment would be found to lack competency if there were an attempt to deny consent. Physicians are not always willing to honor the patient's autonomy when it requires them to sacrifice the patient's best interest, although, in ethical and legal theory, they should do so. Sometimes, though, providers use the competency determination as a way to balance their obligation to adhere to the principle of autonomy with their obligation to adhere to the principle of beneficence. Where those ethical principles lead to conflicting obligations, a finding that the patient is incompetent may be a way out of the ethical conundrum.

IV. INCOMPETENT PATIENTS

A. Introduction and General Principles: Substituted Judgment and Best Interests

Once a determination has been made that a patient lacks the decisional capacity to make a particular health care decision, there must be some alternative method established to make that decision. Because the preservation of autonomy is the principle underlying the rule that patients are entitled to make their own decisions, the alternative decision-making method must be one that protects the autonomy of the patient by carrying out decisions that are consistent with the values and interests of the patient. To serve this end, the decision made on behalf of an incompetent patient should be the decision the patient would make if only that patient were competent for a moment and could see herself in her current condition, including her current state of incompetence. The correct decision is the one the patient would make, not the one the rest of us would make under similar circumstances or the one that the providers, or others, think would be best for the patient.

This principle has come to be known as "substituted judgment," although that name is misleading. The goal is not to substitute anyone's judgment for the patient's judgment, but to figure out what health care the patient would actually choose if the patient had the capacity to exercise her own judgment. The principle of substituted judgment ought to apply in all cases where (1) decisions must be made on behalf of incompetent patients, and (2) there is some way to know what decision the patient, if competent, would make.

The principle of substituted judgment creates many practical problems. For one thing, it requires the assumption of the counterfactual premise that the patient could act competently while viewing herself as incompetent. It also requires that there be some decision maker who is authorized to make this substituted judgment, and that there be a way for that person to find out what choice the patient, if competent, would make. The principle of substituted judgment thus requires that the decision maker—who might be a family member, a health care provider, or a court—follow some process to evaluate the evidence to determine what the patient would actually decide.

Some argue that individual patients' values inevitably change when they become incompetent, and that making decisions for a patient based on the values that patient had before becoming incompetent would undermine, not serve, the principle of substituted judgment. Some aging patients, for example, may say that their life won't be worth saving when they become blind, or incompetent, or unable to hear, or unable to walk—but they may change their minds when they find themselves with those disabilities and realize that life is still worth living. Similarly, perhaps patients who say that they do not want to live without any cognitive ability might feel differently (whatever that may mean under those circumstances) once they start to lose that ability. Of course, the very fact of the incompetence makes it impossible to know whether that is true; and that fact, some argue, makes the application of the principle of substituted judgment logically impossible.

If the principle of substituted judgment cannot be applied to make a health care decision for an incompetent patient, the decision maker must apply the best interest principle as a back-up. Under the best interest principle, the decision maker must make the health care choice that is best for the patient. But what does this mean? Does it mean to do what the surrogate decision maker would do under the same circumstances? What most people would do under the same circumstances?

Ultimately, applying either the principle of substituted judgment or the best interest principle involves resolving many uncertainties—including uncertainties about what the patient would desire and what is in the patient's best interest. To the extent that any substituted judgment is informed by the fact that the decision maker has values and interests that are similar to those of the patient, the principle of substituted judgment begins to look a lot like the best interests principle. Analogously, the application of the best interest principle, when it considers the values of the particular patient in question to determine what is in that patient's best interest, begins to look much like the principle of substituted judgment. In the end, both principles may yield the same results in most cases. Although the choice between the substituted judgment test and the best interests test is very important as a matter of theory, it may mean little as a practical matter.

B. Advance Directives and Family Consent Laws

Although the law governing health care decision making for the incompetent traditionally has been developed in the courts, over the last few decades the common law increasingly has given way to statutory law, primarily through what has become known as advance directive legislation. Initially, this legislation provided that patients, while competent, could sign living wills (now generally called "individual instructions") or other documents that would instruct decision makers to make particular health care decisions if they were called upon to do so after the patients became incompetent. These documents made it much easier to apply the substituted judgment principle, at least with regard to those decisions contemplated by the patient.

Legislatures also created other forms of advance directives, like durable powers of attorney for health care, which allowed competent patients to appoint particular people to make decisions on their behalf should they become incompetent. More recently, states have adopted more general advance directive statutes, some based on the Uniform Health Care Decisions Act, which combine the basic elements of living will legislation and durable power legislation. These newer statutes also include general provisions describing the standards to be applied in health care decision making for incompetent patients, and also family consent provisions, which provide a default priority list of those who may make health care decisions in the absence of any advance directive.

1.   The Rise of Living Wills

Beginning in the 1960s and the 1970s, many people became concerned about the potential abuses of powerful new forms of life-sustaining medical treatment. Frightened by the "treatment" provided to Karen Quinlan, whose life was sustained by a ventilator but who was given no chance of regaining consciousness, people began to search for a way to avoid a similar fate. Within two years of the first press reports of the Quinlan case, several states had adopted statutes that formally recognized certain forms of written statements requesting that some kinds of medical care be discontinued. These statutes, generally referred to as "living will" statutes, provided a political outlet for the frustration that accompanied the empathy for Ms. Quinlan.

The statutes, which still provide the governing law in many jurisdictions, differ in several respects. In some states living wills may be executed by any person at any time (and in some states they may be executed on behalf of minors), while in other states they require a waiting period, and may not be executed during a terminal illness. In most states they are of indefinite duration, although in some states they expire after a determined number of years. Some statutes address only the terminally ill, others include those in "irreversible coma" or persistent vegetative state, and still others provide for different conditions to trigger the substantive provisions of the document. In many states, living wills are not effective while the patient is pregnant, and they do not apply to the discontinuation of nutrition and hydration.

Some states require the formalities of a will (usually, two witnesses) for the living will to be recognized by statute, while other states require different formalities (for example, a notary). The statutes generally relieve physicians and other health care providers of any civil or criminal liability if they properly follow the requirements of the statute and implement the desires expressed in a legally executed living will. Some of the statutes also require that any physician who cannot, in good conscience, carry out those provisions, transfer the patient to a physician who can. The statutes also provide that carrying out the provisions of a properly executed living will does not constitute suicide for insurance purposes.

Some states provide that a living will that is valid where it was executed is also valid in that state. In any case, while a living will that is executed without the formalities required by the state law where it will be carried out will not have the effect given to those documents by statute, it may still provide valuable help to families, health care providers, or a common law court attempting to discover the healthcare wishes of the patient. It is hard to know whether the absence of litigation over living wills means that these documents are working well or not at all.

2.   The Next Step: Durable Powers of Attorney for Health Care

Powers of attorney have been available over the past several centuries to allow for financial transactions to be consummated by agents of a principal. A power of attorney provides that the agent designated shall have the right to act on behalf of the principal, and historically the power was used for matters related to property, and not for health care or other purposes. At common law, a power of attorney expired upon the "incapacity" of the principal. This was necessary to assure that the principal could maintain adequate authority over his agent. As long as a power of attorney expired upon the incapacity of the principal, however, the power of attorney had no value in making medical decisions. After all, a competent patient could make health care decisions for himself; there was no reason for him to delegate authority to an agent.

Over the past several decades it became clear that the value of the power of attorney could be increased if it could extend beyond the incapacity of the principal. For example, as an increasing number of very elderly people depended upon their children and others to handle their financial affairs, it became important that there be some device by which they could delegate their authority to these agents. For such principals it was most important that the authority remain with their agents when they became incapacitated and not before that when they were still competent. The Uniform Probate Code was amended to provide for a power of attorney that could be durable; that is, a power of attorney that would remain in effect (or even become effective) upon the incapacity of the principal if the document clearly stated that. It was never clear whether the Uniform Probate Code durable power provision, which was adopted in every state, applied to health care decision making, and today the vast majority of states have adopted statutes that explicitly authorize the execution of durable powers of attorney for health care decisions.

Although the legal significance of a durable power of attorney for health care is defined by each state's durable power statute, in her concurring opinion in *Cruzan* Justice O'Connor suggested that there may also be a Constitutional right to have an effective durable power of attorney. She commended those several states that have recognized "the practical wisdom of such a procedure by enacting durable power of attorney statutes" and she suggested that a written appointment of a proxy "may be a valuable additional safeguard of the patient's interest in directing his medical care."

3. The Development of the Uniform Health–Care Decisions Act

The Uniform Health–Care Decisions Act (UHCDA), which has been adopted, at least in part, in more than a dozen states and has been highly influential in others, substantially alters the form and utility of living wills and durable powers, and it provides a method of making health care decisions for incompetent patients who do not have advance directives of any sort.

The UHCDA takes a comprehensive approach by placing the living will (which is renamed the "individual instruction"), the durable power of attorney, and a family consent law together in one statute. Further, the statute integrates the current living will and durable power into a single document. The

UHCDA provides a statutory form, but it also explicitly declares that the form is not a mandatory one, and that individuals may draft their own form that includes only some of the kinds of instructions permitted in the unified form.

The new "individual instruction" can apply to virtually any health care decision, not just the end-of-life decisions to which living wills are typically applicable. The Uniform Act also makes the execution of the unified document very easy. It has no witness requirement, and it does not require that the document be notarized. The drafters of the model act concluded that the formalities often associated with living wills and durable powers served to discourage their execution more than to deter fraud, which was their original purpose. In fact, there has never been a reported legal claim that an advance directive was a fraud; that worry, reasonable in the case of some wills, has never been an issue in the case of living wills.

The UHCDA anticipates that there will be a specific decision maker for the patient. There is also a residual decision making portion of UHCDA that applies only in cases where there is no applicable individual instruction or appointed agent. While it provides for a common family hierarchy of decision makers for decisionally incapacitated patients, it also provides that the family can be trumped by an "orally designated surrogate." Thus, patients can effectively orally appoint decision making agents who previously could only be appointed in a writing signed pursuant to a rigorous process. In the same manner, a patient may orally *disqualify* someone who otherwise would be entitled to make decisions on her behalf. If someone does not want his crazy older brother or his cruel aunt making health care decisions for him, he need only tell his treating physician. Thus, in essence, any health care decision will be made by the first available in this hierarchy:

(1) the patient, if the patient has decisional capacity,

(2) the patient, through an individual instruction (i.e., a living will),

(3) an agent appointed by the patient in a written power of attorney for health care,

(4) a guardian,

(5) a surrogate appointed orally,

(6) the highest name on the list of family members and others who can make health care decisions on behalf of the patient.

Note that some states have provided a priority list that is different from this one.

The drafters of the UHCDA make it clear in their comments that one purpose of the statute is to assure that these intimate health care decisions remain within the realm of the patient, the patient's family and close friends, and the patient's health care providers, and that others not be permitted to disrupt that process. The court would very rarely have a role in any decision making under this statute, and outsiders (including outside organizations) who do not think a patient is adequately protected have no standing to seek judicial intervention.

The UHCDA explicitly provides that the decision maker (whether an agent, guardian or surrogate) should make a decision based on the principle of substituted judgment (i.e., on the basis of what the patient would choose, if that patient were competent) rather than the best interest principle. If it is impossible to apply the substituted judgment principle, the statute would apply the best interest principle.

4.   Family Consent Statutes

Over the past century it became standard medical practice to seek consent for any medical procedure from close family members of an incompetent patient. There is no common law authority for this practice; it is an example of medical custom (and good common sense) being subtly absorbed by the law. The President's Commission suggested five reasons for this deference to family members:

(1) The family is generally most concerned about the good of the patient.

(2) The family will also usually be most knowledgeable about the patient's goals, preferences, and values.

(3) The family deserves recognition as an important social unit that ought to be treated, within limits, as a responsible decision maker in matters that intimately affect its members.

(4) Especially in a society in which many other traditional forms of community have eroded, participation in a family is often an important dimension of personal fulfillment.

(5) Since a protected sphere of privacy and autonomy is required for the flourishing of this interpersonal union, institutions and the state should be reluctant to intrude, particularly regarding matters that are personal and on which there is a wide range of opinion in society.

It is difficult to determine whether the resort to close relatives to give consent is merely a procedural device to discover what the patient, if competent, would choose, or whether it is based in an independent substantive doctrine. Although it seems essentially procedural—the family is most likely to know what the patient would choose—many courts are willing to accept the decisions of family members even when there is little support for the position that these family members are actually choosing what the patient would choose. Of course, consulting with family members also neutralizes potential malpractice plaintiffs; this factor undoubtedly accounts for part of the longstanding popularity of this decision making process.

Over the past decade most states have enacted "family consent laws," either as a part of the adoption of UHCDA or independently of it. These family consent laws authorize statutorily designated family members to make health care decisions for their relatives in circumscribed situations. These statutes often apply to a wide range of health care decisions (including, in most cases, decisions to forgo life sustaining treatment), although sometimes they apply only when there has been a physician's certification of the patient's inability to make the health care decision, and sometimes they are limited to particular kinds of treatment (e.g., cardiopulmonary resuscitation). In addition, family consent laws often provide immunity from liability for family members and physicians acting in good faith, and judicial authority to resolve disputes about the authority of the family members under the statutes.

The definition of "family member" and the position of each family member in the hierarchy vary from state to state. In some states those in a long term spouse-like relationship with the patient are included in the list of family members who can make decisions for the incompetent patient; in some states they are not. Some lists include a residuary class of anyone who knows the values, interests and wishes of the patient, just in case no one else on the family list is available. Some states list the physician as the residuary decision maker; some provide for no residuary decision maker. Some states give a general guardian top priority; some states do not. Some states allow the statutory surrogate to make any health care decision; some states put some kinds of decisions (like discontinuing nutrition and hydration) off-limits to appointed surrogate decision makers.

5. POLST: Physicians' Orders Regarding End-of-Life Care

By custom, health care institutions and health care workers caring for patients rely on orders given by the health care professional, usually a physician, responsible for the patient's treatment. Recognizing this custom, some patient advocates argue that the most practical way to effectively protect a patient's interests at the end of life is to incorporate the patient's health care decisions into a physician's order. One way of doing this is to incorporate those decisions into a Physician Order for Life Sustaining Treatment (POLST). POLST forms (called "scope of treatment" orders in some cases, and Medical Orders—"MOLST"—in New York) may include information about a patient's decisions with regard to resuscitation orders, the extent of appropriate medical intervention, the use of antibiotics and other pharmaceuticals, the provision of nutrition and hydration, the desired place of treatment (home, hospital, or nursing home), the identity of the authorized health care decision maker, and other relevant issues likely to arise in each case.

POLST forms are generally entered in the patient's medical record after the physician has discussed all of the relevant issues with the patient, the patient's family, the agent or surrogate authorized to make health care decisions, and others. The POLST form may include a summary of the values and goals of the patient that form the basis of the order, and the nature of the discussions that gave rise to the order. The patient or the patient's decision maker may be asked to countersign the order so it is clear that it represents the agreed view of the patient and the provider. In order to assure that these forms are not lost in the patient's chart, they are often printed on distinctively colored (usually bright pink or bright green) paper. Such orders can be recognized by state law (as they are in a few states), or by institutional or community policy. While some argue that the POLST movement improperly turns decisions that ought to be made by patients into orders that must be signed by physicians, and thus undermines patient autonomy, supporters argue that it is just a practical way of making sure that patients' decisions are really carried out in health care institutions, where the culture requires a provider's approval before anything can be done.

C. Making Decisions Concerning Life Sustaining Treatment When There Is No Advance Directive

In the first instance, a health care decision made for an incompetent patient is made by the patient's appointed surrogate or a close family member. If anyone disagrees with that decision, the issue may end up in court, although recent statutes have discouraged judicial intervention. The role of the court depends on the law of the state, and the court may be called upon to (1) determine who has the legal authority to make the decision, or, less commonly, (2) make the decision itself. In In re Guardianship of Schiavo, 916 So.2d 814 (Fla.App.2005), the court was authorized to make the decision itself under Florida law. That extremely controversial case pitted the patient's husband (who wanted treatment removed after his wife had been in persistent vegetative state for more than a decade) against her parents (who believed a miracle could still save their daughter and who thought that removing nutrition and hydration was immoral). If the court addresses the first question—who has authority to make the decision—it will be called upon to analyze state law to determine the proper decision making locus. If the court is called upon to make the second substantive decision, it will consider evidence to determine how to apply the substituted judgment standard, or, if that is impossible, the best interest standard. In either case, the court will generally not order the removal of life-sustaining treatment unless that decision is supported by clear and convincing evidence.

The clear and convincing evidence standard has been applied differently by different courts, but it has the effect of causing the court to err on the side of life. If the evidence is in equipoise, the court will decide against removing life-sustaining treatment. Courts have rejected the application of a criminal-like "beyond a reasonable doubt" standard in these civil cases, but the consensus is that something more than the ordinary civil "more likely than not" standard is required. A few courts have determined that the clear and convincing evidence standard can be met only when there is evidence that the patient made a formal statement indicating his wishes before he became incompetent. Most courts receive a wider range of evidence on that issue, and they entertain testimony on the patient's diagnosis, prognosis, life history, ethical beliefs, religious beliefs, and attitudes toward health care, life and death, before they make the decision.

Some courts apply the purely subjective substituted judgment standard only when the wishes of the patient have been clearly expressed. When there has been no such unambiguous expression, though, they apply a standard that allows the discontinuation of life-sustaining treatment when there is some trustworthy evidence of the wishes of the patient and the burdens of treatment or the continuation of life outweigh the benefits of doing so. In those cases where there is no trustworthy evidence of the patient's view whatsoever, those courts permit the discontinuation of treatment only if the burdens markedly outweigh the benefits. Some state courts make it easier to remove life-sustaining treatment when the patient is in persistent vegetative state with no chance for any recovery than under other circumstances.

Very early writing about the discontinuation of life-sustaining treatment sometimes focused on distinctions that are now universally seen to be irrelevant. For example, philosophers and lawyers agree that the difference between active and passive conduct is illusory, and virtually every act can also be cast as an omission. The act of removing a ventilator from a patient can also be seen as omitting continued ventilator support of the patient. Similarly, there is no meaningful ethical or legal distinction between withholding and withdrawing care. There is no obligation to continue any form of medication of a patient, for example, just because it was initiated earlier. If there were, providers might be reluctant to start that form of treatment in the first place. Similarly, early distinctions between ordinary and extraordinary care, and between heroic and normal treatment, have now been abandoned as meaningless.

While the distinction between providing nutrition and hydration and providing other forms of care has been rejected by most bioethicists, physicians, and professional organizations, there is a minority that views it to have continuing value, and, as indicated above, it persists in the law of many states. Many living will statutes specifically exclude the performance of any procedure to provide nutrition or hydration from the definition of death-prolonging procedures, for example, and thus do not extend any statutory protection to those who remove nutrition or hydration from a patient. This may be because we associate nutrition and hydration with the most basic care society owes all of its members, and because we are worried about the effect allowing their discontinuation would have on the society-wide respect for life. Alternatively, this may be the result of the religious divide that is so obvious throughout our national debate over end-of-life care.

As a general matter, courts (including the Supreme Court in the *Cruzan* case) have not seen any difference between nutrition and hydration and other forms of medical treatment. In *Cruzan*, the Chief Justice reviewed those state cases that have treated nutrition and hydration just like any other form of medical care, apparently with approval. In her concurring opinion in that case, Justice O'Connor cited the AMA Ethical Opinion on withholding or withdrawing life-prolonging medical treatment to support her proposition that "artificial feeding cannot readily be distinguished from other forms of medical treatment." In his dissent, Justice Brennan states without reservation: "No material distinction can be drawn between the treatment to which Nancy Cruzan continues to be subject—artificial nutrition and hydration—and any other medical treatment."

V.   NEVER–COMPETENT ADULTS AND THE "RIGHT TO DIE"

If it is difficult to apply substituted judgment to determine what treatment a recently incompetent patient would choose, it is more difficult still to apply that test to an adult who has never had decisional capacity. In such a case, usually involving treatment proposed for a seriously mentally retarded or developmentally disabled patient, it is difficult for the decision maker to serve the value of autonomy because the patient has never been able to develop (or, at least, express) life values, interests, and wishes that can be applied in a meaningful way. Some courts have concluded that it still may be possible to apply the principle of substituted judgment because it still may be possible to identify the wants and needs of the patient, while others have required decision makers to move immediately to the best interest standard, although those desires of the incompetent patient that can be identified might still be considered relevant in determining what is in the best interest of the patient.

As is often the case, the selection of the substituted judgment or best interest test seems to hinge on the underlying substantive result that the court finds appropriate. Courts which apply the substituted judgment standard are more likely to permit the discontinuation of life-sustaining medical treatment, while courts that adopt the best interest standard are more likely to require continued treatment, often on the default ground that the preservation of life is always in the patient's interest.

One state, New York, has now resolved the question of which standard to use by statute. The New York statute allows a guardian appointed by a court (and, more recently, a family member otherwise authorized to make a decision) to make all health care decisions on behalf of an incompetent mentally retarded or developmentally disabled adult patient as long as the decision maker also considers the patient's wishes, "including moral and religious beliefs." The statute maintains New York's bias in favor of continued treatment, and it allows the guardian or family member to terminate life-sustaining measures only if the patient is terminally ill, permanently unconscious, or suffering from an irreversible life-long disease. It permits the discontinuation only if the treatment would impose an extraordinary burden on the patient, and it imposes additional requirements before a decision can be made to remove artificially provided nutrition and hydration. Essentially, the New York legislature responded to the public uproar that followed a case in which the state court found that it was legally impermissible to remove treatment from a patient who had never been competent, even where the patient's family, the patient's physicians, and the hospital's ethics committee all agreed that the treatment should be discontinued, and even where the patient was suffering as a result of continuing treatment.

Disability groups have joined with right-to-life groups to oppose most efforts to remove life-sustaining treatment from mentally retarded and developmentally disabled patients. Those groups argue that society undervalues the lives of the disabled, and that it is too easy for a guardian or family, already burdened by the patient's care, to discontinue life-sustaining treatment even when doing so fails both the substituted judgment and best interest tests. Some disability advocates have suggested that the solution lies in substantively rigorous standards that must be met before treatment can be removed under these circumstances, and others believe that the solution lies in judicial review of all such decisions, even when that is not required when the same decisions are made for other incompetent patients. Still other advocates argue that the mentally retarded and the developmentally disabled should have the same right to die as others, and that the imposition of additional legal conditions in their cases is unethical, and, perhaps, unconstitutional. The New York statute has survived at least one legal attack based on the due process and equal protection clauses of the Fourteenth Amendment and the argument that it was void for vagueness.

VI. CHILDREN, NEWBORNS, AND THE "RIGHT TO DIE"

A. Making Decisions for Children

Children, by definition, are not legally competent to make most health care decisions, although there are exceptions made by statute law and common law in every state, and there is a Constitutional exception for those engaged in making reproductive decisions. The law has determined that the principle of autonomy is not served if children make health care decisions; rather, their values and interests are more likely to be protected if those with more wisdom and experience make those decisions until the child is mature enough to do so herself. As a matter of general course, children become adults at age 18, although some states have lowered that age under some circumstances. Until a child reaches that age of majority, the default position is that the child's parent, or, where appropriate, a legally recognized guardian, is authorized to make health care decisions for the patient.

The 18–year–old age of majority has been criticized as being too high, at least for most children in most circumstances. In Europe and elsewhere, the age is almost always lower, and a great deal of research suggests that children's decision making skills, at least when they are supported by an appropriate adult sounding board, mature at some earlier point, perhaps around 14. That research also suggests that individuals do not reach full decision making maturity, even as a matter of physical development, until the middle of their 20s—something every parent of a teenager knows.

In an effort to address the issue that the age of medical consent is often set too high, the law has developed different ways to allow some children to make their own health care decisions. Almost all states recognize that a child can become an "emancipated minor," and thus entitled to all of the decision-making authority of adults, under circumstances that are usually established by statute. Emancipation statutes require a court order, which may be granted when a minor is married, serving in the military, managing his own affairs, supporting himself, or some combination of these and other factors. Ordinarily, emancipated minors must be over 16, and, of course, they must have figured out how to file and litigate a fairly complex lawsuit to achieve that status.

Many states also recognize the "mature minor" doctrine, usually by common law rather than through statute. A child is a mature minor when that child has the same decisional capacity an adult would need to make a particular health care decision. While the mature minor doctrine can result in litigation over a child's legal status, it sometimes allows a health care provider to recognize the decision-making authority of a child—usually a teenager—without resort to the courts.

The state, exercising its long-recognized parens patriae power to protect the health and welfare of its children, may intervene and take health care decision making with regard to a child away from the parents. When a state determines that a parent's decision is inconsistent with the health and safety of their child, it may seek an injunction and a judicial determination of the proper treatment for the child, or it may seek legal custody of the child under state abuse and neglect laws. When a court makes a health care decision for a child, there is a debate over whether it should apply the doctrine of substituted judgment or the doctrine of best interest. In either case, courts try to consider the wishes of the children when those children are old enough to be able to participate in some meaningful way in the decision making process. Thus, as you might expect, decisions involving very young children are more likely to involve a pure best interests analysis, while decisions involving older teenagers are more likely to depend upon a substituted judgment test. Some courts have declared that they can use only the best interests test in these cases, but even those courts take the children's values, wishes, interests, and declared choices into consideration when applying that test. In these circumstances it becomes very difficult to distinguish the substituted judgment and best interest tests.

When cases are prosecuted as child abuse and neglect cases, they must follow the state procedure and substantive law that applies to those cases. Medical neglect includes the failure to seek appropriate health care for a child, and a parent found by clear and convincing evidence to have medically neglected a child may lose legal custody to the state. The loss of legal custody does not require the loss of physical custody, and in the course of a child neglect action a court may order the child to undergo the questioned treatment but still leave the child in the physical custody of the parents, as long as they do not obstruct the treatment. A determination that a child is medically neglected does not necessarily mean that parents are culpable, although over the past two decades a few states have imposed their separate criminal abuse and neglect laws, or even involuntary manslaughter laws, on Christian Scientist and other parents whose decisions not to seek treatment for their children have resulted in the deaths of those children.

Whether applying ordinary civil law, abuse and neglect law, or some other species of state law, when a court is called upon to order medical treatment for a child against the wishes of a parent—usually the result of a complaint made by a health care provider, family member, or friend—the court will generally balance the Constitutionally recognized parents' interest in making health care decisions for their children with the child's interest in receiving proper health care and the state's Constitutionally recognized interest in protecting the life and health of the child. The court will generally consider such factors as the relative maturity of the child, the chance the treatment will actually provide relief for the child, the side effects of the treatment (both physically and psychologically), and the length and quality of life both with and without the proposed treatment.

In some cases, this balancing is very easy. This is true, in the words of one court, "when the treatment is relatively innocuous in comparison with the dangers of withholding medical care." When a Jehovah's Witness child needs a blood transfusion, for example, universally it will be ordered, even over the parents' heartfelt and sincere objections, when it is likely to return the child to full health with no serious adverse consequences. Competent adults may choose to be martyrs to their faiths, but the law does not allow them to impose that martyrdom on their children, even if their children say they would choose the same path. The goal of the law is to assure that those children live to become competent adults, when they can choose that martyrdom if they wish to do so.

The issue becomes tougher when the benefits of treatment are less clear, the burdens of treatment are more severe, and the child is older and more able to participate in the decision making process. For example, courts have often applied this balancing test in cases where medical authorities seek to provide highly painful, disabling cancer treatments that have an uncertain chance of leaving the child with anything like a normal life. If a child is almost certain to die as a result of the cancer without treatment, but has a 20% chance of two-year survival after an excruciatingly painful and disfiguring series of surgical interventions and long-term chemotherapy, a court engaged in the balancing process could come out either way. In these cases, courts are likely to give especially serious consideration to the wishes of the patients if they are older children who have been through cancer treatment protocols before, and the result of the balancing generally is not to order treatment when the child strongly opposes it.

Most of the cases in which courts are asked to order treatment against parental objection involve the parents' religious objections to the treatment, and, not surprisingly, many of those cases involve Jehovah's Witnesses and Christian Scientists. Most states have promulgated statutes that provide that "spiritual healing" per se cannot constitute child abuse or neglect for purposes of the state's criminal or child protective services statutes. In fact, for some time the existence of such protections were required as a condition of receiving some forms of federal funding. Some litigants have argued that these statutes violate the establishment clause of the First Amendment or the equal protection clause of the Fourteenth Amendment because they give a preference to Christian Scientists and protect their "recognized practitioners" in ways that they do not protect others. On the other hand, perhaps these statutes simply reflect our society's attempt to balance the protection of children through the reach of abuse and neglect laws into the domain of family autonomy, on one hand, with parental power, on the other. Most commentators who have considered the issue have determined that these statutes are not Constitutional, at least as they are applied to civil abuse and neglect proceedings, although the Supreme Court has not definitively resolved the issue.

While courts regularly address questions where parents refuse to consent to treatment that health care providers believe is medically necessary, they also sometimes confront the reverse situation. In one case, the District of Columbia Court of Appeals approved a DNR order for a neglected, comatose two-year-old child who was born "neurologically devastated." The child was taken from his drunken mother after he had been left alone for days without his necessary heart and lung medication. The mother opposed the hospital's request that the child be given DNR status. Applying the best interest (rather than the substituted judgment) standard, the court recognized that the mother might be criminally liable for homicide if the child were to die, and it thus disregarded her request that there be aggressive attempts at resuscitation. Many other states have also faced cases in which parents who might be charged with serious homicide crimes have opposed a state's request that treatment be discontinued when it is likely that the discontinuation of treatment will result in the death of the child.

B. Newborns and the "Right to Die"

If it is difficult to apply the principle of autonomy to an incompetent adult who has been competent, and nearly impossible to apply that principle to serve an incompetent adult who has never been competent (but who has expressed likes and dislikes), it is simply impossible to apply that principle to a seriously ill newborn. The principle of beneficence, then, must become primary. The obligation of health care professionals and institutions is to do what is in the best interest of the infant. Because parents are presumed to be acting in the best interest of their children, parents of seriously ill newborns traditionally were permitted to determine whether their infants would receive treatment, and what kind of treatment that would be. Thus, historically, if a parent of a newborn with some severe birth anomaly determined that it would be best for that child not to receive life-sustaining treatment, that determination was honored even though it would result in the certain death of a child whose life otherwise might be saved.

The question of what treatment must be provided to a seriously ill newborn, however, has proved to be more complex. Philosophically, the difficulties arise out of the fact that parents of newborn infants with serious defects may not always act entirely in the best interest of those infants. While parents undoubtedly feel responsibility for all of their children, a seriously ill newborn is likely to be a particularly great financial and emotional drain on his parents and the rest of the family. Given the risk that the parents' interest will be in conflict with the newborn's best interest, some have suggested that the state should not defer to parents in making health care decisions for their newborn children.

In addition, questions surrounding seriously ill newborns often require a determination of whether life-sustaining treatment should be forgone. It is hard to know just what it would mean to say that death is in the best interest of a newborn who may be capable of so little brain activity that he will never feel any sensation whatsoever. This raises a fundamental and extremely difficult bioethics question: can non-existence ever be better than existence? More precisely, is it possible for any court to determine the value of life for a child who will never be able to feel any joy, but also never be able to feel pain or unhappiness? What can best interest mean under such circumstances? It may turn out to be just as meaningless to apply the best interests standard as to apply the substituted judgment standards under these circumstances.

These are precisely the kinds of questions that have been answered by families and providers at the local institutional level within our health care system for decades. Indeed, that is exactly what had been happening throughout the country; the ultimate determination generally was left to the parents, who were heavily influenced by the hospital medical staff. Without much public attention, and with discussion limited primarily to medical and ethical professional organizations, somewhat different standards were applied in somewhat different institutions. Then came the Baby Doe case.

Baby Doe was born on April 9, 1982, in Bloomington, Indiana. He was born with Down's Syndrome and a fistula which would require repair to allow the baby to consume nutrition orally. The parents decided not to authorize the necessary surgery, and the baby was given phenobarbital and morphine until he died, six days after birth. During Baby Doe's short life he was the subject of a suit commenced by the hospital in the local children's court, which refused to order that the surgery be done. The Indiana Supreme Court denied an extraordinary writ that would have had the same effect, and the attorneys for the hospital were on their way to Washington to seek a stay from the United States Supreme Court when the issue was rendered moot by Baby Doe's death. Baby Doe presents a very stark case for philosophical and jurisprudential analysis. The physicians refused to do the operation because the parents refused to consent. The parents refused to consent because their child had Down's Syndrome. If the child had not been born with Down's Syndrome, he would have been provided the surgery.

Several political groups, including right-to-life groups and advocacy groups for the developmentally disabled, were outraged by the circumstances of Baby Doe's death. Looking for some way to redress this issue, the federal Health and Human Services Department hit upon Section 504 of the Rehabilitation Act of 1974, which forbids any agency receiving federal funds from discriminating on the basis of handicap. In March of 1983, the Secretary of Health and Human Services issued emergency regulations to assure that no hospital would avoid providing necessary treatment for seriously ill newborns. These regulations provided for federal agents to immediately investigate any hospital that put at risk the life or health of a handicapped infant by denying that infant life-sustaining treatment. The regulations also required large signs describing federal policy in all maternity and pediatric wards and newborn nurseries, and they established a toll-free number to report violations of the regulation.

Pediatricians challenged the regulations and successfully argued that they were defective because they had not been issued after the notice and comment period required by the Administrative Procedures Act. DHHS then proposed slightly revised regulations ("Baby Doe II") and invited comments. In early 1984 the new final regulations ("Baby Doe III") were issued. These regulations were based on the articulated substantive principle that "nourishment and medically beneficial treatment (as determined with respect to reasonable medical judgments) should not be withheld from handicapped infants solely on the basis of their present or anticipated mental or physical impairments."

Under the final regulations the federal government maintained its investigatory and enforcement roles, state child protective services agencies were required to develop processes to investigate cases of non-treatment of seriously ill newborns, and individual institutions were encouraged to establish "Infant Care Review Committees" to review appropriate cases. Once again providers challenged "Baby Doe III" and the Supreme Court, without any majority opinion, ultimately determined that the regulation had been improperly promulgated.

While the challenge to Baby Doe III was wending its way through the courts, principals on both sides of the issue agreed to a compromise that was turned into the Child Abuse Amendments. This statute is considerably weaker than the regulation that preceded it, but it does condition each state's receipt of some federal child abuse prevention funding on the maintenance of procedures for dealing with reports of the medical neglect of newborns. Regulations issued under the Child Abuse Amendments interpret "medical neglect" to include "the withholding of medically indicated treatment from a disabled infant with a life threatening condition." Further, the regulations provide that the " 'withholding of medically indicated treatment' means the failure to respond to the infant's life threatening conditions by providing treatment (including appropriate nutrition, hydration, and medication) which in the treating physicians' ... reasonable medical judgment will be most likely to be effective in ameliorating or correcting all such conditions."

Under this statute, no doctor has an obligation to provide care to an infant who is "chronically and irreversibly comatose," when the treatment would "merely prolong the dying process" of the infant and not ameliorate or correct the underlying medical problem (and thus be futile, as defined by the statute), or when the treatment would be "virtually futile" and "inhumane."

Although the issue increasingly rarely arises in the judicial setting, courts are loathe to allow infants who can be "saved" to die. In the United Kingdom, on the other hand, there is far more toleration of a family decision to discontinue treatment of an infant with a "brain incapable of even limited intellectual function." The British courts are willing to consider explicitly the quality of life of a seriously ill newborn, as was demonstrated in one case in which treatment was not required for a newborn because "[c]oupled with her total physical handicap, the quality of her life will be demonstrably awful and intolerable." Treatment decisions made for seriously ill newborns depend heavily on the values of the physicians involved in the decision making, and upon the locality in which the decision is made.

In the United States, national attention focused on the issue of the appropriate treatment of seriously ill newborns once again in 2003 as a consequence of a high profile Texas lawsuit in which parents were awarded a judgment of over $60,000,000 (including thirty million for actual damages for medical expenses and thirteen million in punitive damages) against a health care institution for failing to follow parents' instructions to withhold life-sustaining treatment from their infant. When labor started, the parents and the treating obstetrician agreed at the hospital that the prognosis for the four-month premature baby who was about to be born was so awful that the physicians would institute no "heroic measures," that they would not attempt to resuscitate the baby, and that the infant would die shortly after birth if it were not stillborn. The child, Sidney, was born alive. Another obstetrician attended the birth following a shift change, however, and he followed the hospital policy that required resuscitation of a baby with Sidney's birthweight. The baby suffered a very serious brain hemorrhage. Seven years later, when the parents' informed consent battery claim and the accompanying negligence claim went to trial, the court found, that "the hemorrhage caused Sidney to suffer severe physical and mental impairments.... Sidney ... could not walk, talk, feed herself, or sit up on her own.... Sidney was legally blind, suffered from severe mental retardation, cerebral palsy, seizures, and spastic quadriparesis in her limbs. She could not be toilet-trained and required a shunt in her brain to drain fluids that accumulate there and needed care twenty-four hours a day. The evidence further demonstrated that her circumstances will not change."

The Texas Supreme Court, in Miller v. HCA, 118 S.W.3d 758 (Tex.2003) rejected the hospital's argument that their actions were required by the Child Abuse Amendments and the regulations promulgated to enforce them. On the other hand, that court determined that all of the medical decisions were made during the course of a continuing emergency that ensued after the birth, and that the emergency exception to the doctrine of informed consent permitted the hospital to intervene and provide care without consent of the parents during that emergency. In the end, a combination of the medical bias in favor of treatment and the application of the emergency exception to the doctrine of informed consent left the parents without a remedy against a hospital that failed to do what its agents had promised the parents it would do. Under the Texas law, the court determined, no hospital will ever face liability, in the absence of extrinsic negligence, for the decision to resuscitate or not resuscitate any baby, without regard to what request for treatment is made by the parents.

Some parents may now be reluctant to give birth to babies that may have severe anomalies in American hospitals because they reasonably fear that the hospitals will feel obliged to do everything they can to save every baby's life. Although the Baby Doe regulations themselves do not impose serious burdens on those who seek care in the newborn nursery, the fear that arose as a result of the debate over the development of those regulations still controls decision making in neonatal intensive care units.

VII. FUTILITY

Treatment is scientifically futile (or medically futile) when it cannot achieve the medical result that is expected by the patient (or by the family) making the request. As a general matter, scientifically futile treatment need not be offered or provided to a patient. A seriously ill cancer patient need not be provided with laetrile, a useless drug that has been popularized by those who would prey upon desperate patients and their families, even if that treatment is requested and even if there is no other proven treatment. A child with a viral illness need not be prescribed an antibiotic, even if the child's parents request one, because, as a matter of science, the antibiotic will not be effective in treating that illness. Doctors need not do a CAT scan on a patient with a cold, even if that is what the patient wants, because there is no reason to believe that there will be any connection between what can be discovered on the scan and the appropriate treatment of the cold. As a general matter health care providers, who are trained in the science of medicine, are entitled to determine which treatments are scientifically futile, and there is no ethical or legal obligation to provide scientifically futile care to anyone.

A harder question arises when a patient requests treatment that is not scientifically futile, because it will have the effect it is designed to deliver, but that is, in the opinion of the health care provider, ethically futile. Treatment is ethically futile if it will not serve the underlying interest of the patient. For example, some providers believe that it is ethically futile to keep a patient's body aerated and nourished when that patient is in persistent vegetative state. These health care providers believe that it is beyond the scope of medicine to sustain mere corporeal existence. Some health care providers believe that it would be ethically futile to engage in CPR under circumstances in which the most that can be accomplished through that intervention would be to prolong the patient's life by a few hours. For some patients and their families, though, every moment of life, every moment of corporeal existence, is a precious gift from God that must be highly valued. For those patients and their families, the fact that the requested treatment will merely prolong the dying process is not a good reason to discontinue it; indeed, that is a powerful reason to embrace that treatment. It is hardly surprising that families disagree with physicians over what constitutes ethically futile treatment from time to time, and the law has been pressed to determine how to deal with such disagreements. Because the dispute is over a matter of ethics, not a matter of science, there is no obvious reason to adopt the provider's perspective, rather than the family's, as the ethically "correct" one.

The AMA has formally determined that physicians have no obligation to offer treatment options that "will not have a reasonable chance of benefiting their patients." On the other hand, when physicians deny patients treatments that have no chance of helping their patients, the AMA believes that those physicians should explain their positions by reference to general ethical principles and recognized standards of care rather than by reference to the term "futility," which has taken on so many different meanings in so many different contexts.

Texas has dealt with the issue of futility by statute. That statute provides that if a physician refuses to honor a patient's request that life-sustaining medical care should be initiated or continued, whether that request is made by the patient, and authorized decision maker, or an advance directive, the patient must be fully informed of the right to appeal the physician's decision to an ethics committee, and there must be an adequate opportunity for the patient and the patient's family to prepare for this unusual ethics committee appellate review. In the meantime, the treatment must be continued pending the ethics committee decision. If the committee upholds the doctor's decision, that physician, with help from the facility's staff, is required to transfer the patient within ten days to a provider who will carry out the patient's wishes. If no one can be found to take the patient and provide the requested care, the original provider may discontinue providing that care after the ten days have elapsed unless a court extends the ten-day period based on a finding that "there is a reasonable expectation that a physician or other health care facility that will honor the patient's directive will be found if the extension is granted." The Texas statute also creates a registry of those who are willing to assist in the transfer of patients whose treatment has been found to be futile, although the list that has been developed includes very few names.

Some states with statutes modeled on the Uniform Health–Care Decisions Act also have statutory provisions that provide that physicians need not provide futile care. That Act provides that "[a] health-care provider or institution may decline to comply with an individual instruction or health-care decision that requires medically ineffective health care or health care contrary to generally accepted health-care standards applicable to the health-care provider or institution." Really, the Texas statute differs from the Uniform Act only in providing a clear procedure for resolving these issues and an authoritative and conclusive endpoint for disputes.

In the absence of a relevant statute or meaningful common law directed to this issue, individual providers are left to address the issue in individual cases. Many hospitals have adopted futility policies, some of which do include reference to the institutional ethics committee in a role as mediator, facilitator, or quasi-appellate decision maker. As a general matter, those policies require that futility decisions be made and recorded through a process that is transparent, and include a full discussion with the patient or the patient's authorized decision maker. Most institutions have no policy on futility, apparently leaving the issue to patients and their families in consultation with their health care providers. In the absence of any institutional policy, individual providers are left to determine their own ethical and legal obligations, and, in many institutions, an ethics committee may still be available for consultation and advice. A few states have statutes, and some institutions have policies that address futility regarding particular kinds of treatment, like those involving "do not resuscitate" orders or orders regarding artificial nutrition and hydration. These statutes and policies cover a very thin sliver of the futility cases institutions and providers confront.

In its essence, the application of the doctrine of futility is a limitation on the application of the principle of autonomy, which generally governs health care decision making. As those who oppose the limiting principle inherent in the doctrine of futility suggest, autonomy and patients' choices are not really honored if they are recognized only when patients want to refuse treatment, and not when they want to continue treatment. The application of the doctrine of futility to limit treatment is also complicated by the financial implications of the doctrine, which, in some case, could save money for some institutional health care providers. Those opposed to the application of the principle are concerned that payers and providers beholden to them will stretch the doctrine to save resources, and not to serve the other and more defensible values. They are also concerned that doctors do not appreciate the quality of life of the disabled or religious values of families and patients. Those who support the application of the doctrine of futility to limit treatment may also recognize the low benefit-cost ratio of the life-sustaining treatment that is usually the subject of the debate, but their primary argument is that futile care is simply beyond the scope of appropriate medical care and thus beyond the obligation of the health care provider.

CHAPTER 6

PHYSICIAN–ASSISTED DEATH

I. INTRODUCTION—AND A WORD ON TERMINOLOGY

Over the past several years the law, like many other social institutions, has engaged in a vigorous discussion of the propriety of physician-assisted death. In large part an extension of the debate over whether and when life-sustaining medical treatment can be withdrawn, the debate over physician-assisted death is a consequence of medical developments that allow patients to be kept alive—even without continuous medical intervention—under conditions that some patients find worse than death itself. While scholars have come to use the more neutral and descriptive phrase, "physician-assisted death," the popular debate over this issue also sometimes refers to the process as euthanasia (literally "good death" in Greek, treated as the killing of another person for that person's benefit), which can be either active (an affirmative act resulting in the death of another) or passive (an omission resulting in the death of another). Others, usually opponents of the practice, call it "mercy killing" while supporters refer to the same practice as "physician aid in dying" or "death with dignity," which is also the name attached to the two state statutes that permit this conduct in the United States. Those two statutes, promulgated through the initiative process in Oregon and Washington, permit "physician-assisted suicide," a practice in which a physician aids a patient, commonly by providing a prescription for a lethal dose of medication, who then takes an act with the intent that his death result, and which results in his own death.

Like many other issues in bioethics, physician-assisted death is particularly controversial in some religious circles. Many religious groups believe it is wrong for any person to intentionally cause his own death under almost any circumstance, while others believe that the choice ought to be made by the patient, and that there are circumstances where a decision to take one's own life is morally permissible. In the secular discussion of this issue, advocates for permitting physician-assisted death usually take a utilitarian course, while natural law theorists oppose it and deontological thinkers are ambivalent about how to protect the patient's autonomy while showing full respect for every person's life.

As a legal matter, physician-assisted death (and, more broadly, euthanasia) have been regulated in different states in a number of ways, but most forms of physician-assisted death remain illegal (and, in fact, criminal) in the vast majority of states. First, an affirmative act that is intended to cause the death of another and does so generally constitutes murder. Because consent is not a defense to a homicide crime, the fact that the patient asked to be killed is not relevant to the criminal legal analysis. Second, many states criminalize assisting suicide or aiding and abetting suicide. The fact that the aid was requested by the patient, or is conducted for the benefit of the patient, or is a medical process conducted by a doctor, are each legally irrelevant because none of them provides a defense to this criminal charge. All states have now repealed statutes that made suicide itself illegal. Although those statutes never resulted in the prosecution of a successful suicide, of course, they had often been invoked to prosecute those who unsuccessfully attempted suicide and who had thus committed the inchoate crime of attempted suicide.

II. CONSTITUTIONAL BACKGROUND

In 1997, the Supreme Court unanimously decided two cases testing the Constitutionality of state laws that made it a criminal act to aid another person in taking his own life. In Washington v. Glucksberg, 521 U.S. 702, 117 S.Ct. 2258, 138 L.Ed.2d 772 (1997), the Court reversed a Ninth Circuit en banc determination that Washington's statute prohibiting a person from causing or aiding in another's suicide violated the due process clause of the Fourteenth Amendment. In Vacco v. Quill, 521 U.S. 793, 117 S.Ct. 2293, 138 L.Ed.2d 834 (1997), the Court reversed a Second Circuit determination that the New York law, which permitted a patient to refuse even lifesaving medical treatment but which made criminal an affirmative act that would aid a patient to commit or attempt suicide, violated the equal protection clause of the Fourteenth Amendment.

In applying the due process analysis in *Glucksberg*, the Court's decision hinged on the articulation of the question presented. While the Ninth Circuit had described the question as the existence, vel non, of a due process liberty interest in "controlling the time and manner of one's death," the Supreme Court asked "whether the 'liberty' specially protected by the due process clause includes a right to commit suicide which itself includes a right to assistance in doing so."

The *Glucksberg* majority opinion (although the decision was unanimous, the Court did not unanimously agree on the way to reach that conclusion) begins with a full discussion of the role of this practice in our history, legal traditions, and practices, and the virtually uniform prohibition of any form of assisted death among state legislatures. The Court recognized that there were, in fact, substantive due process rights, and, in dicta, the Court pointed out that it had "assumed, and strongly suggested" that the "the traditional right to refuse unwanted lifesaving medical treatment" was among those rights. Whether physician-assisted suicide was such a right, though, would depend on whether it was "deeply rooted in American history" such that "neither liberty nor justice would exist if they were sacrificed." The Court found that the right, articulated in the terms described above, did not fit in the limited realm of substantive due process rights.

Thus, because the liberty interest asserted was not a fundamental right, the Supreme Court determined that the appropriate Constitutional test to be applied was whether the ban on assisted suicide was rationally related to any legitimate government interest of the State of Washington. The Court concluded that there were four such legitimate interests: (1) the "unqualified interest in the preservation of human life," (2) the interest in protecting "the integrity and ethics of the medical profession," which, on balance, opposed the practice of physicians assisting in death, (3) the interest in protecting vulnerable groups, like the elderly and the disabled, who could be abused if the practice were permitted, and (4) the interest in avoiding the step onto the slippery slope that would lead to "voluntary and perhaps even involuntary euthanasia."

In *Vacco*, the Second Circuit determined that like cases were not treated in like ways because those suffering terminally ill patients who needed continuous lifesaving treatment could end their lives by refusing such treatment, while similarly situated patients who did not require continuous treatment had no way to exercise that same right. The Supreme Court determined instead that there was an historically recognized distinction between assisting suicide and withdrawing lifesaving treatment that had been recognized both in logic and in law. First, as a matter of causation, an affirmative act (like the administration of a lethal dose of medication) is both intended to cause death, and it actually causes death. Terminating lifesaving treatment, on the other hand, merely allows the patient to die of the underlying disease process. In accepting this analysis, the Court formally recognized the doctrine of double effect, which originally developed in theological argumentation. See Section I.B.2 in Chapter 1. The law had recognized, and continues to recognize, a difference between treatment provided with the intent to cause death, and treatment (like pain relief treatment with very heavy doses of narcotics that might enhance the risk of death) that was provided with the intent to ease suffering but might have the secondary effect of causing death. For the court, the "specific intent" of actually causing death provided a sufficient distinction between assisting death and removing lifesaving treatment to meet the rational basis test that was applied.

In the discussion of this issue in the majority opinion, the Court specifically addressed the increasingly common (but still controversial) practice of terminal sedation, in which a patient in intractable pain is pharmacologically induced into a coma and then not provided nutrition or hydration. Without placing a Constitutional imprimatur on that practice, the Court pointed out that it came within the doctrine of double effect because the primary goal of the treating physicians was to eliminate the pain and the hastening of death was merely a secondary effect. The Court's conclusion as to the permissibility of terminal sedation under double effect is contested.

Finally, applying the rational basis test in doing the equal protection analysis of New York's laws prohibiting physician-assisted death, the Court looked to the same four state interests it pointed out in *Glucksberg*. It concluded that the state decision to classify the termination of lifesaving treatment differently than physician-assisted death did, at the least, "bear a rational relationship to some legitimate end."

It is difficult to figure where to find binding precedent in *Glucksberg* and *Vacco*. While the opinion of the court is signed by five Justices, some suggest that Justice O'Connor's opinion represents the view of a larger majority. Justice O'Connor was a bit more reserved in determining that there is no fundamental right in this area, and her concurrence is founded on the two principles—that the law in every state now gives all patients a right to receive all palliative care necessary to alleviate suffering "even to the point of causing unconsciousness and hastening death," and that the issue can be appropriately resolved through the political process in the states. Her writing suggested that the Oregon Death with Dignity statute, while not Constitutionally compelled, is at least Constitutionally permitted.

Constitutional litigation over physician-assisted death has not been limited to claims based in the Fourteenth Amendment. The same year *Glucksberg* and *Vacco* were decided, the Florida Supreme Court rejected the claim that the state constitution's privacy provision afforded Floridians the right to physician-assisted death. The Alaska Supreme Court reached the same result in 2001; but as this book goes to press in 2009, the Montana Supreme Court is considering an appeal from a trial court that did find a state constitutional right to physician-assist-ed death.

The issue has also arisen in common law litiga-tion over state statutes and common law that ap-pears to outlaw physician-assisted death. Most fa-mously, Jack Kevorkian, a Michigan pathologist, challenged Michigan's limitations (both statutory and common law) on physician-assisted death throughout the 1990s. Kevorkian used a suicide machine that allowed patients—one of whom was photographed playing tennis shortly before operat-ing the machine—to end their lives by pressing a button. After several Kevorkian victories in the courts and the Michigan State legislature, in 1999 he was convicted of murder in a trial in which he represented himself. Whatever one may think of his skill as a physician, he was not a very good lawyer. His conviction arose out of his act injecting a lethal dose directly into a man in his early 50s who was suffering from ALS. Showing more courage or (de-pending on your position) disregard for the law than was discrete, Kevorkian broadcast the whole event on national television.

The jury found that Kevorkian's act was not premeditated, and he was sentenced to 10 to 25 years in prison. He was paroled in 2007 after serv-ing eight years. Reactions to his conviction, which was the focus of American bioethics reporting at the turn of the twenty-first century, ranged from relief that this "serial killer" had been removed from society to anguished shock by those who found the conviction utterly "barbaric." In any case, his celebrated trial, along with the *Glucksberg* and *Vacco* cases, threw the issue from the courts to the political branches of the government. The primary locus of the debate in the first decade of the new millennium has been in state legislatures, Congress, and among the voting population in states with the initiative process.

III. STATE LEGISLATIVE DEVELOPMENTS AND THE PUBLIC DEBATE

With the issue neatly placed in the political arena, there ensued a vigorous policy debate over the propriety of physician-assisted death. Libertarian and health care consumer advocacy groups, along with liberal religious groups and some groups designed to advocate for the elderly, supported legislation that would permit physician-assisted death, primarily because it would give patients greater choice in health care. Supporters argued that there was no more intimate and important life decision than the decision that life was no longer worth living. Thus, they argued, respect for individual autonomy requires that each human being be given the option to choose what that person would consider a dignified death, which would sometimes require the use of medications and thus the assistance of the medical profession, which maintains a legal monopoly on the prescription medications that could cause death in the most dignified manner. Advocates continue to argue that the default position ought to be this pro-autonomy libertarian position, and that patients should be permitted this choice unless there is some very good reason not to permit it. Recently a few medical organizations, including the American College of Legal Medicine (an organization of people with both MD and JD degrees), the American Public Health Association, and the American Medical Students Association have taken positions supporting physician-assisted death.

Opponents of physician-assisted death include right-to-life organizations, disability advocates, some religious groups (including Catholic organizations, Islamic organizations, and more traditionally conservative Protestants and Jews), and many mainstream medical associations, including the American Medical Association. These opponents argue that there are many very good reasons for not changing current legislative bans on physician-assisted death. First, many argue, taking a human life—even your own—is morally wrong, and it shows a disregard for human life for society to permit it. In the end, this faith-based argument may be the strongest reason for supporting this view. The advocates fighting legislation legalizing physician-assisted death are also concerned that the least powerful in society—the poor and uninsured, racial minorities, women, those without any close affiliation with other family members, and, most significantly, the disabled—would be the most likely to succumb, perhaps under inappropriate pressure, to physician-assisted death. There is also some concern that physician-assisted death could not be properly limited, and that it would place us on a slippery slope as lawmakers decide which lives are really worth preserving. Some are particularly concerned by the potential effect any law permitting physician-assisted death might have on the relationship between doctors and their patients; they argue that the fact that doctors might use their authority to end patient lives would destroy the respect patients now have for doctors, who are seen as having the unambiguous goal of saving their patients' lives. Finally, some argue that the fact that we know that there is a regular medical practice of limited physician-assisted death even where it is formally illegal makes it unnecessary to change the law.

Physician-assisted death is now legally permitted as a result of the initiative process (where voters can decide, by majority vote, whether to adopt a statute) in Oregon and Washington. It was narrowly defeated in California and Maine. While it appears to be harder to find support for the practice in the majority of states that do not permit the initiative process, over the last few years a few legislatures have come close to passing legislation permitting the practice. Almost all subsequent legislative proposals have been based on the first law to go into effect, the Oregon Death with Dignity Act, which has been in effect since 1998.

The Oregon statute was written to attempt to accommodate many of the issues raised by those who were concerned by physician assisted death. The statute permits a physician to dispense or write a prescription for a lethal dose (which must be taken by the patient himself) only to terminally ill Oregon-resident patients with less than six months to live. The patient must make the request three times, one of which must be in a written document that is also signed by two witnesses who can confirm that the patient is competent, is acting voluntarily, and is not being coerced to sign. The patient must be fully informed of all of the risks and alternatives to physician-assisted death, including the alternative of comfort care, hospice care, and pain control. The patient must be informed that he can withdraw his request at any time. There must be 15 days between the submission of the written request and the second oral request, and forty-eight hours between that second oral request and the act of writing the prescription.

Along the way, the physician is instructed by the Oregon law to obtain a consult with another physician to confirm the diagnosis and the fact that the disease is terminal, and verify that the patient is making an informed, voluntary, and competent decision. In addition, the physician must refer the requesting patient to counseling if the physician believes the patient may be suffering from any mental disorder or depression "causing impaired judgment." The law encourages, but does not require, patients to tell their family members of their choice. Finally, the statute requires the Oregon Department of Health to keep meticulous records, which the State has made available to the public, providing a wealth of information on many aspects of the effect of the law.

Over the first decade during which the Oregon law was in effect, over 400 patients died as a result of taking a legal, lethal dose of medication prescribed under the law. The number of prescriptions written, and the number of deaths that have ensued, have both increased annually over that period. There were about 25 prescriptions written (and about 15 deaths) the first year, and over 80 prescriptions written, and about 60 deaths, in 2008. In some ways, the concerns of opponents of the Act have been proven wrong, although the sample size may still be too small to generalize and some commentators remain concerned about the value of the self-reported Oregon data. Those who choose physician-assisted death tend to be very well educated (60% had at least a bachelor's degree last year), and the burden of the statute did not fall on people of color (98% were White) or the poor (97% had health insurance of some sort, and 88% had private insurance). There is no evidence that those who were disabled prior to their final illness were disproportionally represented among those who were prescribed a lethal dose.

In addition, the statute appeared to meet some of its goals in improving the dying process for residents of Oregon. Almost all patients who died of a legally prescribed lethal dose died at home, while most other deaths occurred in the hospital. Virtually all patients who died under the statute were enrolled in hospice. Oregon doctors who write lethal prescriptions under the statute (and there were about 60 such doctors in 2008) appear to be disproportionately drawn from specialties, like oncology, that are the most sophisticated in providing end-of-life care generally. Since the passage of the Act, more Oregon doctors have undertaken continuing medical education in palliative care. Finally, many patients who have been prescribed lethal doses have decided not to use them. In those cases, the availability of a lethal dose to be used only if life became unbearable may have extended patients' lives, not limited them, although some argue that there could be other explanations for this result, too.

Perhaps surprisingly, most patients do not choose physician-assisted death to avoid pain at the end of life. From the first year of the Oregon statute's existence, patients were much more concerned with loss of autonomy, a decreasing ability to participate in activities that make life enjoyable, and loss of dignity. Fewer than a quarter considered pain a significant factor in making the decision, and fewer than one in thirty said that financial considerations had any effect on their choice.

So, is the policy debate over physician-assisted death resolved by the "laboratory of the states" experiment in Oregon? Hardly. Those who believe that physician-assisted death is morally wrong still believe that. They believe that the Oregon statute has hastened the death of over 400 people who could have lived longer than they did. Some who oppose physician-assisted death also fear that continued familiarization with physician-assisted death will lead to increasing insensitivity to patients at the end of life, and that we will yet step onto the slippery slope described earlier.

On the other hand, those who believe that physician-assisted death will aid patients in avoiding the loss of autonomy and dignity believe that the data from Oregon show the success of this experiment. In the end, the best predictor of whether any advocate believes the Oregon statute has been a success or a failure is the position that advocate took before the statute even went into effect. Those who support physician-assisted death generally believe the Oregon statute has proven their case. Those who oppose it believe the Oregon statute has proven their case.

This ambivalence does not mean that the results of the Oregon experiment have had no effect on the debate, though. Washington voters looked across their southern border and fairly overwhelmingly passed an initiative very similar to the Oregon law in 2008. That statute has run into some implementation problems in Washington, where some hospitals are developing policies that will make it impossible to practice physician-assisted death within those institutions. Because the vast majority of deaths under the statute will take place at home, this may not turn out to be very significant. Before much data was available from Oregon, an initiative was narrowly defeated in Maine in 2000, and the Hawai'i state legislature came close to promulgating a statute in 2002. The concern over the propriety of this kind of legislation (and for its chances of political success in other states), and the common interest in end-of-life care, has also caused advocates on both sides of the issue to work together on pain relief legislation which has been adopted in many states. This legislation is designed to make it more difficult to institute criminal and administrative actions against health care providers endeavoring to provide adequate pain relief, even when the provision of that relief may also hasten the demise of the patient.

The Oregon statute was subject to substantial litigation designed to block its implementation. It also was the subject of proposed federal legislation and federal administrative action aimed at limiting the purpose for which medication could be prescribed by those with DEA licenses. The litigation delayed the effective date of the Oregon law, but it also ultimately confirmed the language invoked in *Glucksberg* and *Vacco* that this issue was one to be decided on a state by state basis through the democratic process. It is likely that we will have a chance to observe that democratic process in this context in many states over the next few years.

IV. THE INTERNATIONAL DEBATE

The debate on physician-assisted death is taking place outside of the United States, too, and it is marked by the same arguments and concerns elsewhere that have been raised here. The vast majority of national laws make physician-assisted death illegal, either directly or indirectly, through general homicide statutes and other criminal laws. The first formal legislative action to legalize physician-assisted death was taken by the Northern Territory's Parliament in Australia in 1995, and four patients availed themselves of the protections in that statute before it was effectively overturned by the National Parliament two years later.

In 2001, the Netherlands, which had first "tolerated" (but not formally legalized) physician-assisted death in 1969, fully legalized the process where patients faced intractable suffering (in the form of pain or otherwise) and had followed appropriate procedural requirements through the Termination of Life on Request and Assistance with Suicide Act. Although the country was divided over the propriety of physician-assisted death (mostly, but not entirely, along religious lines, with Protestant political entities supporting it and Catholic religious and political entities opposing it), there is now strong popular support for the current Dutch system, which depends in large part on the deep Dutch respect for both individual practitioners and the national medical association.

Although the Dutch statute confines euthanasia to certain medical conditions, the practice has expanded. The Dutch supreme court recognized that a defense of necessity to homicide was available for euthanasia for patients who were not terminally ill if the physician took exceptional care in securing consultation with another physician. In addition, although the statute allows euthanasia for a child over the age of twelve with parental consent, the practice has been extended to newborns in a few cases. No physicians have been prosecuted in these cases and a published medical protocol is generally followed. The protocol requires that the diagnosis and prognosis be "hopeless" and that the infant be experiencing unbearable suffering.

Belgium followed the Dutch lead by formally legalizing physician-assisted death under some circumstances in 2002. The Belgian law, like the Dutch law, applies to those in unbearable suffering, whether or not they are terminally ill. The Belgian law imposes a 30–day waiting requirement after a formal request is made by a patient who is not terminally ill, however. Like most physician-assisted death statutes adopted outside of the United States, the benefits of the Dutch and Belgian laws can be extended to teenagers under some circumstances.

Switzerland also now permits assisted death, and, unlike the Netherlands, Belgium, Oregon, and Washington, the assistance need not be provided by a physician or any other health care provider. Assisting suicide, whether performed by a doctor or a lay person, is criminal in Switzerland only if done for "selfish" rather than "altruistic" motives. It is difficult to compare European and American approaches to this issue, because the European statutes often do not clearly distinguish between withdrawing or withholding life sustaining treatment and euthanasia. Much of the data collected in Europe combine information on withdrawing life support and more direct physician assistance in death.

Colombia became the first nation in the Americas to permit physician-assisted death when a majority of its Constitutional Court found that terminally ill patients had a right to seek aid in ending their lives in 1997. Thailand has permitted physician-assisted death by statute since 2007, although the language of the Thai statute, like the language of some of the European statutes, appears to do nothing more than permit a patient to forgo life sustaining care. The intensity of the debate over physician-assisted death has become stronger over the past decade, though, and we are likely to see the national debate in the United States reflected in the international debate, and vice versa.

CHAPTER 7

ORGAN TRANSPLANTATION

I. INTRODUCTION

Legal and ethical issues relating to organ transplantation arrange themselves around two distinct but related considerations. The first is the question of the supply of organs, involving the retrieval of human organs and efforts to increase the supply of transplantable organs. The second is the question of how scarce human organs should be allocated or distributed for transplantation. These questions are considered separately in the discussion that follows. As you will see, however, some of the legal and ethical principles adopted in relation to retrieval of human organs contribute to the inadequacy of the number of organs available for transplantation; and some of the efforts to increase the supply of organs necessarily relate directly to the distribution of those organs.

This chapter focuses on the operation of the U.S. transplantation system and does not address the increasing globalization of transplantation. For some time, individuals from other countries have come to the U.S. for transplantation services, and there has been an issue of whether citizenship is relevant to receiving a scarce organ. More recently, however, the flow of travelers has increased from the U.S. to other nations as U.S. patients try to escape the wait lists in the U.S. The restrictions regarding both acquisition and distribution of human organs described in this chapter do not necessarily apply in other nations, although there are increasing attempts to harmonize requirements across national lines.

II. THE SUPPLY OF HUMAN ORGANS FOR TRANSPLANTATION

While there has been a constant effort to increase the number of organs available, certain restrictions on retrieval of human organs for transplantation depress the supply below what it could be. Public policy rests on several ethical principles that form significant boundaries on the supply of human organs, at least at this time. First, organs are to be treated as a matter of personal property or personal integrity and not as commons owned by the public upon death. Second, life-sustaining organs cannot be relinquished by or taken from living persons. Third, payment for organs presents risks to the moral fabric of the transplantation system. Each of these principles is at play in the legal framework described in the next sections.

A. The Uniform Anatomical Gift Act (UAGA)

1. Structure of the UAGA

The UAGA is a model statute developed by the National Conference of Commissioners on Uniform State Laws. The first version of the UAGA was published in 1968, and substantially revised versions appeared in 1987 and 2006, with some amendments in between. The UAGA is not operational as law unless it is adopted by a particular state; however, every state has adopted some version of the UAGA since its inception. Variations among the state anatomical gift statutes are common and significant, but the UAGA provides a useful general framework for the discussion of common legal issues.

The UAGA has a limited reach. It covers only the donation of organs and tissue upon death (i.e., cadaveric organs). It does not cover donations of non-vital organs by living donors. The UAGA aims at increasing the supply of organs while supporting the primacy of altruism and preserving the rights of individuals to govern the disposition of their own bodies after death. The Act, and the state statutes based upon it, provide for pre-mortem commitment of post-mortem donation by individuals; post-mortem donation by surviving kin; the option of designation of recipient; and immunity for transplant organizations involved in organ retrieval. While the 1987 UAGA provided for "presumed consent" for organ retrieval, the 2006 UAGA eliminated that provision. Many states retain the earlier provision for presumed consent, and that process is treated in a separate section below.

2. Pre-mortem Document of Gift

The UAGA provides a vehicle for the donation of organs through the execution of a "document of gift" by an individual prior to death. The document need not follow any particular formalities. Statements in living wills, durable powers of attorney, testamentary wills, donor cards, and notation on a driver's license are all acceptable. The Act also provides for the execution of pre-mortem document of gift by a legally incompetent individual's guardian or designated health care agent.

If an adult has executed a pre-mortem gift of his or her organs, no further consent or consultation with the surviving family is required. The pre-mortem gift is effective; the surviving kin are barred from revoking or amending the gift; and the organs are to be retrieved in compliance with that document. Prior to the 2006 revisions, only adults could make a valid pre-mortem document of gift under the UAGA. The 2006 Act provides that adolescents (who are emancipated or of the age to have a driver's license) have the authority to make a pre-mortem document of gift; however, in the case of an adolescent who is not emancipated, a parent may revoke the gift upon the child's death and block organ retrieval.

3.   Post-mortem Donation

In the absence of a pre-mortem document of gift, the UAGA provides that other individuals may authorize the removal of the decedent's organs and lists certain classes of individuals who may do so. The first listed category is the agent appointed by the decedent (as in a durable power of attorney for health care). Thereafter, family members are listed in order of priority: first the spouse, then adult children, parents, adult siblings, adult grandchildren, and grandparents. If any member of a prior class is reasonably available to make the donation decision, the next class has no authority. The 2006 version added "an adult who exhibited special care and concern for the decedent" to the list of those who could authorize an anatomical gift, but only if prior classes (i.e., the patient-designated agent or listed family members) are unavailable. Of course, states may modify the list by addition or subtraction or by rearranging priority.

An oral statement of a desire to donate an organ after death does not bind survivors under the UAGA, unless the declarant is terminally ill. It is quite common, however, for surviving family members to try to do what the decedent would have done, although they are not required to do so in this circumstance by the Act.

4.   Immunity

The UAGA provides immunity from civil, criminal, and administrative action for individuals retrieving organs in accordance with the anatomical gift statute or "attempt[ing] in good faith" to comply with the statute. While this is a rather broad extension of immunity, a surprising number of cases have been filed against hospitals and transplant organizations for actions taken in the harvesting of organs, with most of these cases denying defendant's motion for dismissal or summary judgment. Typically, the suits involve disputes over the nature and scope of the family's consent to removal in the absence of pre-mortem gift (e.g., that the hospital removed certain organs that had not been authorized). The Act also extends absolute immunity to the organ donor or donor's estate, declaring that they will not be "liable for any injury or damage resulting from the making or use of the gift."

5. Designated Donation

The UAGA recognizes the right of a donor to designate a cadaveric organ for transplantation for a specific individual or for the use of a specific organization. The recognition of designated donation respects the principal of autonomy of the donor, but it also is believed to have the potential to increase the supply of organs by motivating potential donors to rescue identified individuals in need or to increase their own chances of receiving an organ should they need one. Designated donation of organs, however, has raised significant controversy regarding its impact on the distribution of available organs. See Section III.E, below.

B. Presumed Consent

1. Statutory Provisions

The 1987 UAGA allowed for removal of organs or tissue under particular circumstances without either pre-mortem directive from the decedent or consent of surviving kin. If the hospital or coroner had no knowledge of an objection by the decedent prior to death, or by a person authorized to decide for the decedent, and reasonable attempts to contact such persons had failed, the Act authorized the removal of the organs despite the lack of actual consent.

Rather than relying on a claim that cadaver organs are a commons or publicly accessible, this provision was viewed as "presumed consent." Presumed consent rests on a rebuttable presumption of consent and on data that indicates that the majority of people would consent to organ donation if asked. States that adopted presumed consent provisions made substantial variations: some statutes limited presumed consent to particular tissue (such as corneas and pituitary glands) rather than extending it to solid organs; and some omitted the requirement that there be reasonable attempts to contact surviving family.

The 2006 version of the UAGA, however, removed the provision for presumed consent as a response to litigation challenging the practice as unconstitutional. Some states have repealed their previously adopted presumed consent laws, but others have not.

2. Constitutional Challenges to Presumed Consent

Surviving family members have challenged the nonconsensual removal of tissue and organs as a violation of their Constitutional right to property, with the property right being the family's common law or statutory authority to possess the decedent's body for purposes of disposal. The scope of this common law right is quite ambiguous and had in the past been interpreted as a duty, related to public health concerns, rather than as a right. Two early state cases rejected claims of right on the part of families; but the federal Court of Appeals for the Sixth Circuit recognized the Constitutional claim in the early 1990s, as did the Florida Supreme Court in 2001.

The implementation of presumed consent was undermined by a series of investigative reports in the Los Angeles Times demonstrating that the practice in California had a disproportionate impact on minorities as 80% of coroner autopsies were performed on African–American or Latino individuals and only 16% on white decedents. The articles also revealed that the cornea business was a major source of revenue for the coroner's office, as the tissue was sold to tissue banks, and downstream for the tissue banks as well.

As a result of the articles, families sued the coroner. In Newman v. Sathyavaglswaran, 287 F.3d 786 (9th Cir. 2002), the Court of Appeals held that families have a Constitutionally protected property interest in the bodies of deceased family members and that removal of body parts thus requires due process of law. The *Newman* decision recognizes a State interest in the retrieval and distribution of organs and tissue but does not specify the procedures that would satisfy due process requirements balancing the State's interest and the property rights at issue. The California statute did not require any attempt to contact family members prior to removal, although many state statutes authorizing presumed consent do so require; and the coroner apparently ignored or did not wait a reasonable amount of time for family members to record objections. The California legislature repealed the challenged provision without attempting to amend it to meet due process standards.

C. Payment for Organs

1. Statutory Restrictions

Federal law provides that it is illegal for "any person to knowingly acquire, receive, or otherwise transfer any human organ for valuable consideration for use in human transplantation if the transfer affects interstate commerce." 42 U.S.C. § 274(e). The statute defines human organ as "human (including fetal) kidney, liver, heart, lung, pancreas, bone marrow, cornea, eye, bone, and skin or any subpart thereof." This definition leaves some gaps. It does not cover materials such as semen, ova, and blood, which are bought and sold in rather robust markets. It also does not cover tissue that is taken for research or commercial development rather than for human transplantation.

The federal prohibition is thus quite limited in scope, but it does prohibit the buying and selling of solid organs for transplantation. The federal statute, however, permits "reasonable payments associated with the removal, transportation, implantation, processing, preservation, quality control, and storage of a human organ or the expenses of travel, housing, and lost wages incurred by the donor of a human organ in connection with the donation." The first part of this definition allows for the rather lucrative industry that has grown around the retrieval, processing, and transplantation of human organs, where every service, except for the donation itself, generates revenue. The second part of the definition allows for some payments to individual donors for financial losses incurred in the donation of organs.

The UAGA prohibits the sale of "an organ, tissue, eye, bone, artery, blood, fluid, or other portion of the human body," but the Act applies only if removal occurs after the individual's death. The UAGA allows payments for the professional services listed in the federal statute but does not authorize any payments to the donor or the donor's family.

2. Proposals to Allow Payments for Organs

Proposals to allow the purchase of human organs for transplantation appear to be gaining momentum. Federal legislation has been introduced to allow for the study of compensation systems for post-mortem removal of organs. Some states have experimented with payments to donors for specific expenses or through tax credits. Private donor matching groups are pushing the boundaries of payments allowable under the current federal statute for travel, housing, and lost wages.

Proponents of payment for organs argue that such payments will increase the supply of organs and avoid the loss of life on the current wait lists. Proponents also argue that the sale of organs would better respect individual liberty and autonomy, would better serve justice by distributing some of the wealth created in the organ transplant system to the individuals contributing the raw material, and would better serve equality of opportunity by increasing access on the part of minority individuals. Some advocate allowing payment only in the case of cadaver organs but not for intervivos organ transplants.

Opponents of these proposals maintain that less problematical efforts to increase supply, such as increasing the number of living donors, the rate of gifts upon death, and expanding the classes of persons who would be considered dead for purposes of organ donation, should be implemented first. Opponents also argue that payment for organs would result in the commodification of the human body, would exploit the poor for the benefit of the rich, and would raise the social and financial costs of organ transplantation.

D. Living Donors

Individuals donating non-vital organs (such as one kidney or a portion of the liver) have become a very significant source of transplantable organs. A variety of ethical and legal issues arises in the context of retrieval of organs from living human beings, however.

1. Competent Donors

For persons who are competent to consent to organ donation, the ethical issues tend to involve concerns over the voluntariness of the gift. These concerns center both on questions of coercion, especially when the transplant occurs within a family, and on questions of the quality and completeness of the information that the donor receives about the risks of the retrieval surgery as well as the health consequences of living without the donated organ.

Ethical concerns arise as to the level of risk one should be allowed to assume and the informed consent process. Research on the long-term effects of organ removal on living donors is lacking because outcomes for such donors are not now tracked systematically. As more patients with higher risk factors are accepted as living donors, however, some argue that there should be a limit to the level of risk tolerated by and for the donor. Some also argue that the informed consent process be modified to create an independent advocacy team for the donor because of concerns that a single doctor cannot both treat the recipient and get consent from the donor without running heightened risks of incomplete information and coercion.

These ethical concerns may translate easily into legal claims. Living donors may assert claims for failure of informed consent or for malpractice in relation to the assessment of risk factors for specific donors, the acceptance of higher risk donors, or the quality of the medical care the donor receives.

2. Incompetent Donors

Other ethical and legal issues arise when the donor is not competent to consent to organ retrieval. The judicial opinions on the matter of organ retrieval from incompetent patients tend to adopt the decision-making framework used for surrogate health care decisions generally. See Sections IV, V, and VI in Chapter 5 for further discussion of issues relating to surrogate consent for incompetent patients and health care decision making for children.

E. Determination of Death

A core principle of organ transplantation in the U.S. is that life-sustaining organs are not to be removed from living persons. This "dead donor rule" limits the supply of transplantable vital organs. Thus, legal standards used to determine whether an individual is dead influence the supply of organs, and concerns for increasing the supply of organs in turn influences those standards. See Chapter 4.

III. DISTRIBUTION OF ORGANS
FOR TRANSPLANTATION

Human organs for transplant are a scarce resource. In the absence of competitive bidding for organs, other methods are used to allocate available organs among those in need. The distribution of human organs for transplantation raises issues of distributive justice. See Section III in Chapter 1.

Potential organ recipients are not allowed to compete for organs by bidding for them, but access to organ transplantation does depend on the ability of the recipient to pay for transplantation services and the very expensive post-transplant maintenance care needed to overcome rejection of the organ. Those who are not able to pay, either through Medicare (which covers some transplants but not others and only for eligible individuals), Medicaid (which does not cover large segments of the poor population and which pays at levels that are so low that some transplant centers resist doing the procedures), private insurance (which may exclude coverage for transplantation generally or may set caps on payments for medical services or drugs), or out-of-pocket resources (including bake sales and other community fundraising efforts), are not placed on the list to receive an organ.

The transplant distribution system balances a number of sometimes competing goals. Because organ supply depends on donations, maintaining public confidence in the distribution system is viewed as critical and supports efforts to assure the integri-

ty of the distribution system. Concerns relating to
the "survivability" of the organ in transplantation
are acute. Where the odds of the transplant being
successful are low, the organ may be viewed as
wasted. There is, however, a counterbalancing sen-
sitivity to the urgency of medical need, and so, the
likelihood that a potential recipient will die without
a transplant is considered relevant. There is also a
concern for fairness of opportunity among individuals and among particular populations, and apparently neutral policies may have an unintended dis-
parate impact.

A. Federal Law on Organ Distribution and UNOS

The National Organ Transplant Act of 1984
(NOTA) required the federal Department of Health
and Human Services (HHS) to establish a national
Organ Procurement Transplant Network (OPTN)
to organize the retrieval, distribution, and transplantation of human organs. HHS contracts with
the United Network for Organ Sharing (UNOS), a
private, not-for-profit organization, for the management of the nation's organ procurement and distribution system. Federal regulations set standards for
organ distribution, and UNOS develops policies for
review by HHS through an advisory group appointed by the Secretary of the Department. UNOS (and
HHS) also monitor the performance and quality of
transplant centers and organ procurement organizations.

B. Listing Patients

UNOS operates a national registry of patients in need of an organ transplant, and the first step in the process of identifying a specific recipient for a specific organ is the listing of the patient on the national transplant registry. UNOS sets standards and guidelines for the listing of patients, but individual doctors and hospitals decide whether and when to list a particular patient. The time of listing and the patient's medical condition (degree of urgency) as reported by the doctor determine the patient's priority on the wait list.

Patient listing practices vary considerably among transplant centers around the country. Transplant centers in high-competition areas, for example, have been found to be more likely to list patients as being in more urgent categories of medical need. Level of pay (e.g. private insurance v. Medicare or Medicaid) is known to influence listing. Two academic health centers settled, without admitting guilt, claims by the federal government that they manipulated the reports of their patients' health status in order to increase their volume of transplants. UNOS policies and federal regulations have increased the specificity of standards for listing in recent times; but the practice remains somewhat informal and variable; and some claim that the informality, variability, and lack of oversight disadvantage women and minority candidates for transplantation.

UNOS listing policies allow doctors to use non-medical, psychosocial criteria in deciding whether to list a patient for a transplant. Such factors may include those behaviors or social conditions that are believed to affect compliance with medical direction; the availability of therapeutic alternatives to transplantation; and consideration of whether the patient's organ failure was caused by avoidable, injurious behavior on the part of the patient. Generally, there is a concern that psychosocial measures of worthiness are not necessarily evidence-based and may be influenced by stereotypes of particular economic classes, racial groups, or behaviors.

C. Geographic Distribution of Organs

Until a change in federal regulation in 1999, the organ distribution system operated on a regional basis so that organs were generally retained for transplantation in the region in which they were retrieved. This system originally responded to the perceived fragility of human organs in transport and to a belief that retaining organs in the region in which they were donated would encourage higher rates of donation. The regional retention policy, however, resulted in vast disparities in the availability of human organs among geographic regions. The wait times for livers, for example, varied from 136 days to 469 days among geographic regions for patients in a particular status category. Individuals with the resources to do so could move to a region with the shortest waiting time and arrange to be listed and receive a transplant more quickly. Patients with the ability to travel at a moment's notice could be listed in multiple regions. The shift to a national system was intended to level out these wait times and to restore public confidence that individuals cannot unfairly jump the line.

D. Organ Matching

Judgments concerning survivability are medical judgments based on medical and scientific expertise, including data on comparative success. Analysis of comparative effectiveness, however, ultimately involves value judgments as well and may implicate concerns of fairness and justice.

For example, while African–American transplant candidates constituted approximately 37% of the kidney waiting list in 2002 and Caucasian candidates, 54%, Caucasians received 64.3% of the cadaver kidneys transplanted that year and African–Americans, 29.1%. This distribution was, in part, a result of kidney matching policies. As a general matter, the more compatible the recipient and the organ, the more successful the transplant is likely to be. The question is what degree of success is desirable at what cost. Data from 2001, for example, indicated one-year survival rates that varied by the frequency of antigen "mismatch" between the organ and the recipient. Those with a mismatch of 5 antigens had a one-year survival rate of 86.1%; those with mismatch of 4, a 87.5% survival rate; 3, 89.2% rate of survival; and 2, 90.4%. While one may consider a difference in survival rates of 86.1% and 90.4% to be significant, the difference between 90.4% and 89.2% is slight enough to raise questions about whether an allocation system that results in disproportionate distribution to persons by race is justified. UNOS altered its kidney match policy in 2003, and transplants for minority recipients have increased.

Interests in survivability or effectiveness are not uniformly given priority. Patients who are "presensitized" because they have received an earlier unsuccessful transplant, for example, are given priority for another transplant even though the likelihood of success is greatly diminished. UNOS rules also give priority to individuals who have previously donated an organ. In addition, organs from donors under the age of 35 are made available first to pediatric patients before any adult patients, even those with greater medical urgency.

E. Designated Donees

Organ donors may select the recipient under UNOS rules and the UAGA. Designation is permitted as a matter of personal autonomy and as a strategy to increase the supply of organs. Such designations have implications for the operation of the distribution system, however.

1. Campaigning for Organs

Persons in dire need of organs and with the means to do so have often engaged in public campaigns, complete with billboards and television appearances, appealing to potential donors for a life-saving organ. These campaigns may increase awareness of the need for organ donations and have a positive effect on organ donation rates generally. Individual campaigns, however, also undermine the agreed-upon standards for distribution of organs that focus on survivability, medical urgency, and fair opportunity. They may disadvantage the less wealthy and less appealing candidates and particular populations.

2. Paired Donations

Living donors may be willing to donate a non-life-sustaining organ to a member of their own family or a close friend but not to a stranger, although the numbers willing to donate their organs to strangers seems to be increasing. Friends and family are not always matches to one another for organ donation, and so transplant centers are arranging paired donations in which simultaneous transplants are performed and the organs exchanged among unrelated donors and donees, with the result that the desired donee receives an organ although not the one contributed by his or her own donor.

3. LifeSharers

LifeSharers is a private non-profit membership organization in which members get priority for organs donated by other members. LifeSharers members must execute a pre-mortem document of gift that designates LifeSharers members on the UNOS list as the preferred recipient. Only if no member is a suitable match is the organ to be made available for general distribution to others on the UNOS registry. An individual must be registered as a member, and have executed a pre-mortem document of gift with the appropriate designation, for at least 180 days prior to the transplant to be included in the priority list. LifeSharers does not require that members be free of conditions that would make their organs unfit for transplantation. LifeSharers justifies its priority system as a means of increasing donations generally and more particularly as a matter of fairness: while organ donation is voluntary, those who choose to commit to be organ donors upon death should receive priority over those who don't.

CHAPTER 8

REGULATION OF RESEARCH
WITH HUMAN SUBJECTS

I. INTRODUCTION

For centuries, physicians and scientists conducted experiments with human beings using only their own moral compass as a guide. Often, they or their families were the first subjects to submit to these experiments. Complete deference to professional virtue, however, was undermined by developments in the mid-twentieth century. The Nuremberg Trials exposed shocking horrors committed by physicians in the name of medical experimentation in the Nazi concentration camps.

In one of the Nuremberg tribunal's most significant judgments, the court promulgated principles for ethical medical experimentation known as the Nuremberg Code. The Nuremberg Code eventually came to form the foundation for regulation of human research in the U.S., but it initially had almost no influence on medical experimentation in this country.

One of the most influential events in the U.S. occurred in 1966 when Dr. Henry Beecher published a landmark article in the New England Journal of Medicine that detailed abuses conducted in the name of medical research in the U.S. Providing 22 examples of unethical research, Beecher established that incidents of immoral experimentation were not uncommon in the U.S. Documented abuses in the U.S. include the development of surgical techniques through repeated unanesthetized vaginal surgeries on slave women; the injection of live cancer cells into patients at the Jewish Chronic Disease Hospital; the intentional infection of children with hepatitis at the Willowbrook State Hospital; and the U.S. government's radiation experiments on individuals and large populations.

The most infamous incident of research abuse in the U.S., and the one that finally triggered significant governmental action, was the Tuskegee Syphilis Study. The U.S. Public Health Service studied 399 African American men infected with syphilis to observe the natural course of the disease if left untreated. Even after the first truly curative treatment for syphilis was generally available, USPHS physicians refused to offer treatment to most of the subjects and insistently discouraged them from seeking treatment elsewhere. For nearly 40 years, the USPHS condemned these men to the ravages of untreated syphilis and exposed their wives and partners to the disease. The study came to light in 1972, and Congressional hearings in 1973 resulted in the commissioning of the Belmont Report and the passage of the National Research Act which established the basic framework for federal regulation of research.

The Nuremberg Code and the Belmont Report provided the ethical foundation for the standards and process used to regulate research in the U.S. This ethical framework deals with competing norms and straddles several of the approaches described in Chapter 1. Ethical principles applicable to research try to maintain respect for the individual even as they operate within an endeavor whose goal is the common good and whose work requires risk to an individual who may not partake in the ultimate benefits of the research.

The ethical and legal framework for research regulation relies on voluntary consent and automony. At the same time, it distrusts that individual choice is adequate to protect individual subjects and maintain respect for human beings. Beginning with the Code and continuing through the current federal regulations, research with consenting human subjects may proceed only when the risks to the individual subject lie within acceptable ranges. The history and ethical framework of medical research tends to view human subjects as requiring protection; however, protectionist policies at times have worked to the disadvantage of particular populations. See Section IV.C., below.

Tension between the common good (i.e., the furthering of experimentation and new knowledge) and the individual's well-being and autonomy (i.e., human subject protection) challenges the regulation of research. Autonomy and beneficence also conflict where individuals are prohibited from consenting to research because the level of risk is viewed as objectively unacceptable. Regulatory oversight processes, which add costs to research, balance concerns for protection of the individual human subject, the integrity of the research endeavor, and the production of important new knowledge.

II. SOURCES OF LEGAL STANDARDS GOVERNING RESEARCH

Federal regulations dominate standard-setting for the conduct of medical research in the United States; however, state legislation, common law, and standards set by private organizations are influencing the legal framework for research. This section briefly introduces these other standards while the rest of the chapter focuses almost exclusively on the federal regulations.

A. State Legislation

Several states have enacted legislation to govern the conduct of research within their boundaries. The federal regulations do not preempt state laws if state law provides protection for human subjects that exceeds that in the federal standards.

Some of these statutes simply extend the application of the federal standards to all research conducted within the state's borders whether or not it falls within the reach of the federal regulations. A good number of statutes make specific provision for particular issues in the conduct of research, for example, by providing for the terms of proxy consent to research on the part of incapacitated individuals. Many states have enacted legislation to govern particular categories of research, including stem cell research. At least one state has imposed particular requirements on the operation of institutional review boards. Finally, state statutes relating to unfair trade practices and the like may also be applied to specific claims by the subjects of research.

B.   Common Law

Individuals who have been injured in the course of medical research may bring suit against the researchers, just as patients who are injured during the course of treatment may bring suit against their physicians and hospitals. Such suits raise familiar tort issues of duty and causation.

Individuals without physical injury have brought suit claiming that their individual rights have been violated, typically in terms of lack of consent to or unacceptable risk in the research protocol itself. Such cases usually are decided under state common law, drawing primarily from tort and contract, but often incorporating the standards of the federal regulations for the content of those claims.

Grimes v. Kennedy–Krieger Institute, Inc., 782 A.2d 807 (Md. 2001), is the most prominent judicial opinion considering claims of this sort. In *Grimes*, the court held that Maryland common law would recognize the relationship of researcher and research subject as one that creates a duty of care and resultant legal accountability and liability on the part of the researcher. The Court relied on the federal regulations on research to analyze the scope of the duty owed to the research subjects, although some argue that the Court misinterpreted those standards as they apply to children. See Section IV.C.1, below. The Court also noted that the Nuremberg Code "might well support actions sounding in negligence" in such cases, although other courts have rejected reliance on the Code. See Section I.D, below. The Court also held that the consent form created an enforceable "bilateral contract" between the parties.

Research subjects have also brought suit claiming an interest in the products of the research in which they participated. These cases have been resolved on a number of state law grounds, including informed consent and property law as well as the application of the federal regulations. See Section V.B.2, below.

C. Private Organizations

Standards set by private organizations have significant influence on the conduct of research with human subjects and could provide evidence of the standard of care. The most significant of these is the Association for the Accreditation of Human Research Protection Programs (AAHRP), a well-established private accreditation organization. The Association of American Medical Colleges (AAMC) establishes policy for medical research performed in medical schools and has been particularly active in regard to the issue of financial relationships between university-based researchers and industry. Other organizations setting standards for some aspect of research, either directly or indirectly, include the International Committee of Medical Journal Editors (ICJME), representing the leading medical journals in the U.S. and abroad, which requires disclosure of financial relationships and listing of clinical trials in public registries as a condition of publication; and the Pharmaceutical Research and Manufacturers of America, a trade group establishing standards for industry funding of research that have influenced government guidance documents, litigation, and practice.

D. International Standards

International standards for the conduct of medical research include the Declaration of Helsinki, promulgated by the World Medical Association, as well as standards of the host country where the experiments take place. Federal regulations on research recognize the applicability of those standards to research conducted outside of the United States. The relevance of international standards for U.S. common law claims, however, has been controversial, even though some aspects of these international standards have been recognized as part of the "law of nations." See Section VI, below.

III. THE FEDERAL REGULATIONS

A. The Common Rule

Many federal agencies have promulgated regulations to govern research conducted by agency personnel or by researchers with agency grants or contracts. Taken together, these regulations are usually referred to as the "Common Rule" because they are quite similar across agencies, although not identical. The HHS regulations govern the greatest portion of research with human subjects, and so those form the basis for the discussion in this section. The Food and Drug Administration (FDA) regulations differ somewhat from those of HHS and the Common Rule generally. Significant differences between the FDA regulations and the Common Rule are highlighted in this chapter.

B. Coverage

1. Covered Entities

The regulations of each of the federal agencies covers only that research conducted by the agency itself or by researchers funded by the agency. The FDA further regulates research on products, such as drugs and medical devices, that are subject to FDA approval and regulation. Research organizations receiving federal funding file "assurances" with the federal government that detail their compliance with the federal regulations. Assurances filed by universities and other academic research organizations typically include a commitment to apply the federal standards to all research conducted by or within the organization.

Not all research organizations receive federal funding for research, have voluntarily committed to compliance with the federal regulations, or are testing products regulated by the FDA. Thus, federal regulations do not necessarily reach all research with human subjects. Only in states that have extended the federal standards to all research or established additional standards is this research subject to public oversight. See Section II.A., above.

2. Definition of Research

Not all "experimentation" falls within the Common Rule's definition of research. The Common Rule defines research as "a systematic investigation ... designed to develop or contribute to generalizable knowledge." The definition includes social science as well as biomedical research, although certain social science studies that present a particularly low risk of harm to subjects may be subject to relaxed levels of review.

Inquiries that are neither "systematic" nor "generalizable" are not research under this definition and are not subject to these regulations. Application of these terms is not entirely clear in every circumstance. Furthermore, an activity that does not fit within the Rule's definition of research at its start may develop over the course of time into a systematic study that will contribute to generalizable knowledge. One way to understand the Common

Rule's definition of research is to apply it to common situations.

a. Clinical Innovation

A physician treating an individual patient may decide to use an intervention that is not approved or ordinarily used for the particular purpose because of preliminary evidence or an educated intuition that it would be effective with this patient. That treatment would be considered "clinical innovation" and may be colloquially referred to as experimentation. It would not be considered a systematic study to produce knowledge that would be generalizable to other patients, however, and is not subject to review under the federal regulations governing research. This scenario is common in many medical contexts, including the use of chemotherapy that has not been approved for use in particular cancers but shows some promise; the modification of a surgical technique to accommodate unusual circumstances; or the adaptation of a medical device to the body of a particular patient.

These innovations may spread out in a way that reaches the thresholds of systematization and generalization when the one-time innovation becomes more frequent and data begins to be collected. The tipping point between clinical innovation and research is not always clear, but the distinction is significant. Only research not clinical innovation is subject to the federal regulations. FDA restrictions on the use of unapproved drugs, however, may restrict clinical innovation in certain circumstances and require a formal research protocol that complies with its regulations on research.

b.   Quality Improvement Studies

The requirement of generalizability is key in deciding whether an organization's studies of its own care procedures and outcomes as part of its quality improvement or patient safety efforts constitute research. So long as the information gained is retained for the use of the single institution, it is unlikely that the quality improvement studies are subject to the federal regulations. When institutions aggregate and standardize their studies and share and compare results, however, such quality improvement research generally triggers the requirements of the federal regulations.

The application of the federal standards to this type of research is quite controversial and is seen by some as impeding the gains of quality improvement and patient safety activities. On the other hand, proponents of gathering this research within the mantle of the federal regulations argue that this is the only reasonable interpretation of the regulations; that human subject protection can always be seen as an impediment to research but is valuable nonetheless; and that the review processes can be performed expeditiously.

3. Human Subjects

a. Definition

The Common Rule applies only when the research is performed with the participation of human subjects. The Common Rule defines human subject as "a living individual about whom an investigator . . . obtains (1) Data through intervention or interaction with the individual, or (2) Identifiable private information."

Intervention and interaction are defined broadly. Intervention, for example, includes both physical contact, such as the drawing of blood, and the type of activities common in behavioral research that alter the subject's environment or engage the subject in an activity.

b. Human Tissue and Medical Records

Studies using medical records and human tissue fall within the reach of the federal regulations, if the medical records include "identifiable" information or if the tissue includes "identifiable" specimens, even if the records and tissue are already available and interaction with the individual directly is not required. The issue, then, is whether the information or tissue is identifiable. Federal guidelines provide researchers with procedures that will adequately code previously acquired tissue and records so that they are no longer tied to a particular, identifiable person. If the records or specimens meet these standards, the study is exempt from the federal regulations, although the guidelines recommend that all protocols involving medical records or stored tissue be reviewed to assure that they are exempt. See discussion of biobanks in Section V.A in Chapter 3.

C. Institutional Review Boards

Federal regulations rely largely on a privatized effort, placing responsibility for reviewing and monitoring research on the research organization itself. The regulations require that research be reviewed by an institutional review board (IRB). Most IRBs are created by and operate within the particular research organization. Some IRBs are freestanding and provide IRB services under contract to specific researchers or research organizations; and at least one state has established a "public IRB" which is available to review research protocols for small research organizations. Whether intra-institutional or contractual, IRBs must meet the standards established in the Common Rule.

1. IRB Composition

The research organization appoints members to its own IRB. The federal regulations provide that an IRB must have at least 5 members, although most university IRBs have dozens of members. The regulations further provide that membership must be diverse in race, gender, cultural background, experience, and expertise; and must include persons with competencies relevant to the IRB's work. An

IRB must include at least one member "whose primary concerns are in scientific areas" and at least one member in "nonscientific areas." In practice, IRB membership is drawn largely from among scientists and physician researchers and almost exclusively from among employees of the organization. An IRB must include at least one member who is not affiliated with the research organization to bring an outsider's perspective to the workings of the board, however. Some question whether this requirement is effective when many IRBs have no more than a single unaffiliated member and provide minimal training to that individual.

2. IRB Duties and Authority

The organization's IRB must review all proposed research to assure that it complies with federal requirements before the research begins. The review process generally involves examination of the research protocol (which describes the study), the informed consent documents, any materials that will be used to recruit subjects, and other documents. The process can be interactive, with the board asking the principal investigator (the researcher responsible for directing the project) to modify the study or documents prior to final approval.

The IRB can subject certain types of studies identified by HHS as presenting minimal risk to research subjects to a streamlined "expedited review." In addition, the federal regulations exempt a defined range of educational testing, observations, and surveys from the application of the regulations' standards, but IRBs typically require that the investigator submit the research protocol to the IRB so that it can perform a quick review to assure that the particular study is actually exempt.

In addition to the initial review and approval process, the IRB must have an effective system for "continuing review." Continuing review is meant to assure that studies continue to meet federal standards and the terms of the IRB's initial approval as the research progresses. The IRB looks especially at the development of unanticipated risks to subjects, the early emergence of particularly positive or negative results that make the risk of continuing the study unwarranted, and the implementation of subject recruitment and consent.

Other administrative levels of the research organization may subject any IRB-approved study to further review and may disapprove research already approved by its IRB; however, the institution may not approve research that the IRB has not approved. The IRB may also suspend or terminate approved ongoing research where the IRB's continuing review or other reports indicate that the study is failing to meet the requirements set by the IRB or has raised other concerns.

D. Governmental Oversight

The federal government engages in some limited direct examination of the performance of research organizations and their IRBs. The federal Office of Human Research Protections (OHRP) enforces the HHS regulations through investigation of complaints, periodic audits of individual organizations, and self-reporting of incidents or problems by research organizations. In an exceptional period of enforcement from 1999–2000, the Office for Protection from Research Risks (OPRR, the precursor to OHRP) found twenty universities, including some of the most prestigious research universities in the nation, to be in substantial violation of the federal regulations. OPRR suspended federal funding of all research at those universities for periods ranging from several days to several weeks. The wave of suspensions has dissipated, although they still occur on a rarer and smaller basis, but their compliance effect lingers.

IV. SUBSTANTIVE FEDERAL STANDARDS

The federal regulations establish the criteria that IRBs must use in reviewing and approving research with human subjects. The three primary requirements relate to (1) risks of harm to the subjects; (2) informed consent of the subject or proxy; and (3) selection of persons as subjects. The standards also require that attention be paid to the privacy of the subjects and the confidentiality of the data collected or used.

A. Risk and Safety

The federal regulations set limits on the types of research to which an individual may consent. They do not permit consenting adults to participate as subjects in research if the risks to the subject are not reasonable in relation to the importance of the outcomes expected of the research or the anticipated benefits to the subjects, if any. The regulations also require that risks be minimized.

Risk accounts for both the severity of potential harms to subjects and the probability that the identified harm may occur. Even the smallest probability of quite severe harm, for example, presents a significant risk. IRB review typically considers a wide range of harms beyond physical harm, including the risk of psychological, social, economic, and legal harm to the individual. The identification and evaluation of risks can be quite subjective.

Subjecting persons to any risk in poorly designed studies is unacceptable as no gain in knowledge will be produced by the study. Thus, the IRB must assure that a study is well-designed from a scientific perspective so that it will produce valid results justifying the participation of human subjects.

The regulations do not require that there be any benefit to the subjects themselves. In reality, even where a particular protocol is testing an intervention with strong potential for therapeutic benefit, any specific individual may not receive this benefit, either because the intervention ultimately proves to be ineffective or because the subject may be randomly assigned to a control group that does not receive the experimental therapy.

Studies typically require randomized allocation of subjects to different arms of the study so that some subjects receive one therapy and others another. Randomization is often essential to produce valid results, but it also may present risks to subjects. Some have argued that randomization is an unacceptable risk unless the state of knowledge about the compared treatments is at a point of "clinical equipoise" in which there is no consensus on the comparative merits of the treatments. A second and related issue of ethically acceptable risk in research design is the use of a placebo arm in a study. Some argue that this design is absolutely essential even where a treatment of some effectiveness exists, and others that it is always unethical. Notions of acceptable and unacceptable risk also form a key boundary for the approval of research involving certain populations such as children. See Section IV.C.1, below. Continuing review monitors changes in the risk-benefit balance during the course of a study. See Section III.C.2., above.

B. Consent

The federal regulations provide significant detail concerning issues that must be addressed in the information given to the subject in the course of seeking the subject's consent. In turn, IRBs spend a good deal of time reviewing the forms that will be used to communicate with the subject during the consent process and to document the subject's consent. The federal regulations specifically provide that their consent requirements do not preempt other federal or state laws that require that more information be provided. The requirement that only freely consenting individuals may be used as subjects in research continues throughout the course of the study as every research subject has the right to withdraw from a study at any time.

1.   Coercion and Undue Influence

Voluntary consent requires the subject to act freely without coercion or undue influence. Some situations, for example where potential subjects are institutionalized and live under the control of others, raise obvious issues of coercion; and the federal regulations require the IRBs to pay special attention to these circumstances. See Section IV.C., below. Other situations also raise concerns over coercion and undue influence.

In Abigail Alliance for Better Access to Developmental Drugs v. von Eschenbach, 495 F.3d 695 (D.C. Cir. 2007), for example, plaintiffs challenged FDA regulations that prohibit the use and distribution of unapproved drugs being studied in Phase I of the drug approval process, except in the context of an IRB-approved study. (Phase I drug trials are the first trials of a drug in human beings and focus on testing the safety of the drug on a very small number of subjects, typically between 20 and 30 people. Phase II and Phase III trials expand the focus to effectiveness and use progressively larger numbers of subjects. Finally, Phase IV trials typically occur after the drug has been approved, but continue to study the performance of the drug in the largest numbers of individuals across longer periods of time.)

Although the FDA had established some narrow exceptions to its prohibition in the context of particular life-threatening conditions under its ''compassionate use'' policy, plaintiffs argued that these exceptions were so narrow as to deny their constitutional rights to make their own medical decisions. The D.C. Court of Appeals rejected the claim, but the FDA later expanded access to such drugs.

The FDA justified its policy in part as a rational balance between early access to drugs and the goal of reasonably assuring that the drugs are safe and effective by restricting their use to research subjects. The case clearly had implications for the research enterprise. If an individual with a terminal disease could get an experimental drug in a Phase I trial without enrolling in an approved research protocol, which includes a significant chance that the individual will be randomly assigned to an arm of the study that does not actually use the drug, the number of patients who would be willing to enroll in the study would probably decline. If denied access to Phase I drugs unless enrolled in a protocol, however, enrollment could be considered coerced.

Enrollment incentives also present a risk of undue influence when there is significant payment for the time and effort of research subjects, especially for those who are financially distressed. Of course, reducing payment levels to avoid undue influence can take unfair advantage of study participants by failing to compensate them for their contribution to the research. Adjusting payment levels to financial status (paying less to persons who may need it more) to reduce undue influence raises other fairness issues. Similarly, incentives paid to subjects to continue participating in the study through its end, if viewed as disproportionate or excessive, compromise the subject's right to freely withdraw from a study at any time. Financial incentives for continuation and completion, however, can be quite important to producing valid results. See also, Section V.A.1, below.

2. No Consent and Proxy Consent

While the Nuremberg Code requires consent in every case, current federal regulations allow research in some circumstances without the consent of subjects. The FDA, for example, allows research on emergency medical conditions without the consent of the research subject if the research cannot otherwise be accomplished; proxy consent is sought where possible; and the community from which subjects are likely to be drawn is notified of the study. This policy has been quite controversial.

The federal regulations also allow research on legally incapacitated individuals if the subject's "legally authorized representative," defined as the person or body authorized under state law to consent on behalf of the subject, consents. The regulations do not provide further guidance on this subject. See Sections IV.C.1 and 2, below.

C. Selection of Subjects

The federal regulations require that the selection of subjects for research be "equitable" and direct that IRBs be "particularly cognizant of the special problems of research involving vulnerable populations, such as children, prisoners, pregnant women, mentally disabled persons, or economically or educationally disadvantaged persons." The traditional goal has been to protect these populations, especially in light of the long history of abuses of some of these groups in medical research; however, exclusion can itself impose significant harm. If particular populations, such as women generally or pregnant women specifically, the elderly, and children are excluded from research, critical knowledge about the behavior of disease and treatment in bodies that may respond differently may be forgone. Federal policy tries to strike a balance between protecting subjects from harm and encouraging their participation in research for this reason.

1. Children

Federal regulations restrict the level of risk to which children may be subjected during the course of research. These regulations intend to be quite protective of children as research subjects.

The regulations on research divide permissible studies with children into three categories according to the level of risk that is anticipated: (1) "research not involving greater than the minimal risk;" (2) "research involving greater than minimal risk but presenting the prospect of direct benefit to the individual subjects;" and (3) "research involving greater than minimal risk and no prospect of direct benefit to individual subjects, but likely to yield generalizable knowledge about the subject's disorder or condition." Deciding whether a research protocol involving child subjects is permitted under the federal regulations requires what is often a quite subjective analysis of risks and benefits.

"Nontherapeutic research," in which there is no direct benefit anticipated for the individual subject, may be conducted on child subjects only if it falls within either the first or third categories. In the absence of direct benefit to the child, risks cannot exceed minimal risk unless the study is directed toward the disorder or condition shared by the child subjects.

The regulations define studies involving only "minimal risk" as those in which the "probability and magnitude of harm or discomfort anticipated in the research are not greater in and of themselves than those ordinarily encountered in daily life or during the performance of routine physical or psychological examination or tests." The regulations do not specify whether the measuring stick for "daily life" is that of a healthy child or that of this specific child with this specific illness and treatment regimen. If the latter measure is chosen, children who are sick may be subject to more invasive research because diagnostic and therapeutic interventions are part of their daily lives. Although many have argued that the measurement should confine itself to risks experienced by the healthy child, the regulations have not adopted this standard. Not surprisingly, IRBs vary significantly in their interpretation and application of the federal standard for minimal risk.

If the protocol is expected to provide a benefit directly to the child subject, as in the second category, the risk tolerance is expanded. Therapeutic benefit to the child subject is well accepted as a direct benefit, but other more incidental benefits, including hypothetical psychological gains by participating in such activity, are less so.

The third category of acceptable research with children magnifies the problems of risk-benefit analysis. It adopts the ambiguous category of minimal risk, adds the notion of "minor" increase in risk, and requires that the experiences of participating be those the children would be likely to undergo anyway. The regulation then introduces a controversial group identification: i.e., the group of children who have the disorder or condition that the research addresses. Some argue that this factor recognizes a felt mutuality among such children through which they can gain a psychological benefit from participating. Others argue that the classification objectifies a group of children by their illness and subjects sick children to risks that would not be visited upon the healthy.

In *Grimes v. Kennedy–Krieger Institute*, the Maryland Court of Appeals considered the application of these standards to a study of the effectiveness of partial lead abatement in housing. See also Section II.B, above. The court correctly noted that parental consent is irrelevant if the research protocol exceeds the level of acceptable risk outlined in the regulations. The researchers argued that the intermittent blood testing and premises testing provided a direct benefit to the children, as the IRB had suggested in approving the research. The court concluded that the research offered no direct benefit to the children and so was nontherapeutic and, therefore, the study could not be conducted if it presented more than "minimal risk."

The case came to the court on defendant's motion for summary judgment, which the court denied. Since the litigation settled after that decision, there was no trial and no final determination of facts and liability in the case. Many argue that the court's conclusion that nontherapeutic research that presents more than minimal risk is not permissible, even with parental consent, departs from the standards of the federal regulations. In addition, the court's identification of risks and benefits is contested by some.

Finally, the federal regulations provide a process for agency review and approval of research protocols that do not meet federal standards for research with children. While an IRB cannot approve such studies, an agency expert panel may do so if the study addresses a serious problem that affects the health or welfare of children.

2. Mentally Incapacitated Adults

The federal regulations permit research with mentally incapacitated subjects with the consent of the individual authorized by state law to act as proxy. The federal regulations do not provide further guidance on the matter. Several states have enacted legislation or promulgated regulations to govern research with mentally impaired persons. With the incidence of Alzheimer's Disease and other forms of dementia typically associated with advanced age growing apace with the demographics of the U.S. population, research on these disorders has increased.

One area of concern is whether an independent assessment of the decision making capacity of the subjects should be required so that those conducting the research are not the only ones deciding whether the individuals have capacity to give consent. A second issue is the appropriate standard for surrogate decision making; i.e., whether the decision should be made on the basis of the best interests of the subject or as the subject would make the decision if capable of doing so. See discussion of these standards in Section IV.A in Chapter 5. IRBs may also be concerned about the location of the research, and some states have enacted legislation to set standards for research with subjects who reside in mental health facilities.

3. Prisoners

Since 1978, federal regulations have seriously limited research with prisoners as subjects. Procedural requirements focus on IRB review: the IRB approving the study must be independent of the prison and must include at least one member who is a prisoner or prisoner representative. For a wide range of cases, approval by the Secretary of HHS is required.

Substantive requirements address subject matter (only research on incarceration or on conditions particularly affecting prisoners as a class is permitted); recruitment (prisoners must not receive advantages from participating in the study, including favorable consideration in parole decisions); and risk (not to exceed the kinds of risk an unincarcerated individual would accept and no more than minimal risk). These regulations define "minimal risk" differently than do the regulations governing research with children as they specify that the measure is "healthy individuals." See Section IV. C.1, above.

The restrictive federal regulations treat prisoners as a population vulnerable to coercion, because of their complete dependence on prison administration, so that consent is viewed as an inadequate measure of autonomy. Some argue, however, that prisoners may benefit from contributing to society and may repair the social contract damaged by commission of crimes.

V. COMMERCIAL INTERESTS IN RESEARCH

Commercial interests in research appear in the sponsorship of research studies, in the forms of payments to researchers, and in the ownership of the results of research. The presence and influence of these interests have grown over the past two decades on several fronts. First, federal funds for research have not kept pace with the value of the research dollar or the demand for medical technology and pharmaceuticals. In contrast, private funding of research by industry has grown exponentially, especially in the area of pharmaceuticals and medical devices. Second, the marriage of the research functions and marketing functions in industry, in the context of clinical trials of approved medications, raised concerns that marketing was masquerading as research. Third, researchers themselves increased their financial interests in the results of their research either by investing in promising products or by securing patents on products they have produced. Commercialization has raised concerns relating to the protection of human subjects as well as the validity of the results of published research. They have also triggered claims by subjects that they should share in the profits.

Commercial interests in research are often called "conflicts of interests," although they do not all meet the classic legal notion of the term, which describes situations where an agent's commitment to the principal's interests may be compromised by the agent's own interests or the interest of another principal to which the agent is obligated. The use of the concept of conflicts of interest to cover issues related to financial relationships in research is intended to focus on incentives that may compromise the performance of the duties of researcher to research subject (which may meet the classic definition) and the researcher's commitment to the validity of the research. Of course, these duties—to the subject and to the research—may themselves conflict. See Sections I and IV.B.1.

The federal regulations, described in Section V.C. below, adopt the legal notion that particular financial interests are suspect even absent evidence of actual misbehavior or harm to subjects. The structure of the financial relationship constitutes a conflict of interest in and of itself. A conflict exists even without evidence that the researcher behaved badly in choosing among competing interests.

Financial interests have received the most attention in the literature and in the regulations. Other pressures, including the drive for tenure, recognition, accomplishment, and competitive advantage, may also compromise the protection of subjects or the validity of research.

A. Industry Sponsorship of Research

Review studies correlating research results with the source of financial support for research have concluded that sponsorship by industry is significantly associated with pro-industry results. These reviews, however, did not demonstrate that the bias rested in the work of the researchers themselves. The skewed results could be produced instead by certain characteristics of private funding for research. It is likely, for example, that a company would choose to fund only that research that showed substantial prospects of positive outcome for its product. In addition, medical journals may have a selection bias toward selecting studies for publication that have positive rather than ambivalent or negative outcomes and thus contribute to the slant of results in the published literature.

A number of practices observed in industry sponsorship of research have raised particular concerns. These include the ghost writing of published articles by company employees rather than by the listed researcher/author, pressure to exclude negative results, and contracts that give the sponsor the right to suppress the publication of studies producing unfavorable results. Steps have been taken by private and governmental organizations to limit these practices. See Section V.C, below.

1. Industry Payment Practices in Research

Industry-sponsored research studies typically pay the researcher a substantial per capita fee for each person enrolled in the study and an additional fee if the subject continues to participate in the study through its completion. Researchers and sponsors argue that the substantial per capita fees are justified by the efforts required in recruiting, enrolling, and retaining subjects. These fees, however, also may incentivize researchers to be so aggressive in recruiting, enrolling, and retaining subjects that they increase risks to subjects or violate their right to freedom in consent and withdrawal. Some are concerned, for example, that researchers may enroll subjects that should be excluded from the study, either because they bear heightened risks or because their medical status would confound the outcomes of the study, or that researchers may unduly influence subjects to enroll or stay in the study. See also Section IV.B.1, above.

In addition, firms sponsoring research are likely to establish other financial relationships with researchers, paying them for attending or speaking at continuing medical education programs, for serving on advisory boards for the company, and for acting as consultants on particular products. If such payments do not correspond with time and effort actually expended by the researchers, they are viewed as merely purchasing influence. See Section V.C, below.

2. Industry Research, Marketing, and Phase IV Trials

Pharmaceutical products and medical devices are approved by the FDA for marketing and use once they are proven safe and effective to the satisfaction of the federal agency. Preapproval studies for safety and effectiveness are quite limited in scope as they are performed on small numbers of persons, over relatively short periods of time, and on populations that are narrowly bounded by medical condition and medication use. See Section IV.B.1, above. In addition, manufacturers typically submit evidence and seek approval for a single use only.

Once the drug or device is approved by the FDA, three things occur that make further study important. First, the drug or device will be used in populations on which it has not been studied. For example, the drug will be prescribed for elderly persons or for persons taking other medications, populations in which the drug may behave differently than expected from the earlier studies. Second, once a drug is approved by the FDA for a particular purpose, doctors may prescribe that medication for other purposes as well, for example for conditions that may be closely related to the approved use (such as in chemotherapy for another cancer or for the treatment of pain from a different underlying condition) or in circumstances where other doctors are reporting positive results. Third, the drug is taken by larger numbers of people and over longer periods of time, revealing adverse events that were not detectable in the smaller pre-approval trials.

Thus, so-called "Phase IV" clinical trials that study a drug's performance after approval are quite important. The federal government provides very little funding for Phase IV studies while industry provides tremendous funding for these studies.

Several legal and policy concerns arise in the context of Phase IV trials. First, because a great proportion of these studies are conducted by physicians in their private practices, there is a concern that federal standards for protection of research subjects are not observed. Second, payments to doctors may not relate directly to their effort in enrolling subjects and recording and reporting results, and so may actually be illegal incentives to doctors to prescribe the firm's medications to the detriment of the patients and the payers. The federal government has charged some of the sponsors who have provided research payments to physicians in private practice with committing fraud on government health payment systems in some of these cases. Most of these cases have resulted in substantial fines.

B. Ownership of the Results of Research
1. Researcher Ownership Interests

The Bayh–Dole Act of 1980 transferred intellectual property rights in the results of federally funded research to researchers and their institutions rather than having the government alone hold those rights as a commons for the use of all. The Act encouraged researchers and research institutions to form and to enter into joint ventures with for-profit companies for the development and marketing of the products of this research.

The goal of the Act was to assure that federally funded research produce tangible products that would move from "bench" to market as quickly as possible. Universities capitalized on this opportunity by seeking patents on their work and by licensing research products to commercial firms, and the number of patents sought by universities annually increased exponentially. The Bayh–Dole Act also changed the complexion of academic research.

The case of Jesse Gelsinger brought the new financial interests of researchers to public attention. Jesse Gelsinger was 18 years old and had a genetic liver disorder that was controlled with medication. Gelsinger consented to become a subject in research testing gene therapy for the disorder in 1999. Gelsinger died as a result of the procedure. An FDA investigation after Gelsinger's death revealed a number of issues concerning noncompliance with federal regulations. Gelsinger's father sued after discovering that both the researcher and the university had a financial stake in the development of this therapy.

Although reports vary in details, it appears that the university gave a private corporation the exclusive rights to patent the results from the researcher's laboratory and allowed the researcher to control up to 30% of the company's stock, a company he founded, in an exception to the university's conflict of interest guidelines. The university was to receive $21 million to support the research, and the university also owned stock in the company. The lawsuit was quickly settled within just a few weeks of its filing. The influence of the litigation as a cautionary tale for conflicts of interest still persists.

2. Research Subjects' Claims of Ownership Interests

Several cases have tested claims by research subjects that they are entitled to a property interest in the results of research produced with their personal participation, tissue, or medical information. Thus far, the courts generally have been inhospitable to these property claims, but have recognized other claims, such as informed consent and contract.

In Moore v. Regents of the University of California, 793 P.2d 479 (Cal. 1990), the landmark case, the plaintiff claimed that his physician, who was treating him and doing research at the same time, removed his spleen, falsely telling him it was necessary for treatment of his disease and never revealing that his tissue would be used in research. The physician-researcher and the University later patented the cell line established from Moore's tissue; and it is currently available for sale to researchers.

Moore argued that he was entitled to a share of the profits from this patent under a theory of conversion as his property right in his own body had been taken from him. The California Supreme Court rejected this claim for a number of reasons, including that the resultant uncertainty as to the legitimacy of the tissue source would have a negative impact on medical research; that property rights in body parts are traditionally quite limited; and that the cell line was created with the substantial work of the researcher as well as Moore's tissue.

The court instead recognized Moore's claims for breach of fiduciary duty and informed consent based on the doctor's deception. Damages under these theories, however, are likely to be more limited than those for the property claim. It is now routine for consent forms to include a general statement that the patient consents to use of removed tissue for research purposes. See also Section III. B.3.a, above.

Researchers and research organizations may also battle over the ownership, or custody and control, of research raw material, and these conflicts can implicate the rights of individual patients. In Washington University v. Catalona, 490 F.3d 667 (8th Cir. 2007), for example, a physician-researcher and thousands of his former patients claimed that a tissue repository that he had developed by collecting and storing specimens from his surgical patients should move with him to another university. The patients claimed that they were exercising their right to withdraw from research, but the federal appellate court concluded that the donors had donated tissue to the medical school and could not revoke that donation. The court accepted the University's claim that it could continue to use tissue that the donors wished to have withdrawn or destroyed so long as the samples were anonymized. See Section III.B.3.b.

C. Regulation of Financial Interests of Researchers

Several federal agencies have adopted policies or promulgated regulations addressing the issue of the financial interests of researchers. Essentially all of these policies and regulations require that the research organization have a written policy; that there be disclosure of relevant financial interests to the institution; and that there be an internal review mechanism. The federal standards set levels for particular financial interests that trigger these disclosure and review requirements, although these vary among the agencies. Research institutions are likely to set lower levels to trigger their internal review.

Under federal standards or guidance, conflicts of interest are to be "managed," "reduced," or "eliminated" as appropriate. HHS guidance, for example, suggests that the institution should consider reduction of the financial interest, disclosure to prospective subjects, separation of the financial and research responsibilities, additional external monitoring of the research, modification of the roles of particular staff (e.g., requiring that someone else secure consent from the subjects), and change in location for the research (i.e., outside of the institution that holds the financial interest) as methods for reducing or managing conflicts.

IRB members may themselves have financial interests in research. Federal regulations require that any member of an IRB that has "a conflicting interest" in the review of a particular protocol may not participate in IRB review of that protocol except to provide necessary information.

Private organizations (including several medical specialty organizations and the Association of American Medical Colleges) have established standards for handling the financial interests of researchers, and these can become the legal standard of care for research organizations. The International Committee of Medical Journal Editors has recommended standards for the disclosure of financial interests, the prohibition of particular practices such as ghost writing, and the posting of all results of clinical trials as conditions of publication. The Pharmaceutical Research and Manufacturers of America has set standards for payments to researchers on the part of pharmaceutical companies, and the HHS Office of the Inspector General has also issued alerts and guidance for these payments as part of its program on health care fraud.

VI. INTERNATIONAL RESEARCH

The number of investigators conducting clinical trials outside of the U.S. under FDA "investigational new drug applications" increased 16–fold during the 1990s. Most countries have established standards and procedures to govern medical research conducted within their borders. The Declaration of Helsinki, Ethical Principles for Medical Research Involving Human Subjects, first promulgated in 1964 by the World Health Organization and amended several times since then, has had a substantial influence on international legal standards.

In 2008, the FDA amended its regulations to accept drug studies conducted outside the U.S. if conducted "in accordance with good clinical practice." Earlier regulations had required compliance with either the Helsinki Declaration or the laws of the site country "whichever represents the greater protection of the individual." The Common Rule provides that covered research that takes place outside of the U.S. must comply with the Rule's standards unless the Department approves the substitution of the standards of the country where the research actually takes place and then only if those standards "afford protections that are at least equivalent" to the federal regulations. These regulations provide that the foreign laws continue to apply as well in any case.

Developing nations are an attractive site for medical research for several reasons: the lack of medical care makes possible research that requires more advanced stages of the target disease; the nation's population may include large numbers of medication-naïve subjects (i.e., persons taking no other medication that may confound the results of the tested drug); and the practical unavailability of certain medical treatments may be used to justify placebo-controlled trials that would not be acceptable in developed nations. Each of these characteristics, however, raises significant ethical and legal issues for the conduct of such research, especially under conditions of extreme poverty that may increase the opportunity for undue influence and coercion.

Abdullahi v. Pfizer, Inc., 562 F.3d 163 (2d. Cir. 2009), considered the testing of Trovan, an antibiotic, by a U.S. company during an epidemic of bacterial meningitis in Nigeria. As described in the case and in news articles, families and medical workers charge that researchers administered Trovan to children suffering from meningitis without informing the parents of the known serious risks of the drug and that medication known to be effective was available without charge. They further charge that the researchers administered an ineffectively low dose of another antibiotic known to be effective at higher doses to a control group of children to improve the results for Trovan. The families filed suit against the company claiming that the research caused the deaths of 11 children and seriously injured many others.

The appellate court reversed the trial court's dismissal of plaintiffs' claim under the Alien Tort Statute, which provides the federal courts with jurisdiction over tort claims by foreign nationals for violations of the "law of nations" or U.S. treaties. The court held that "nonconsensual medical experimentation on humans" violated a universally accepted norm of customary international law, relying on the Nuremberg Code, the Declaration of Helsinki, and the federal regulations on research. The dissent argued, in part, that it was inappropriate to consider the Nuremberg Code, as it had no independent legal force, and the Declaration of Helsinki, as it is merely a private standard.

VII. STEM CELL RESEARCH

The science of human stem cell research is itself embryonic and currently is characterized more by potential than by results, although the promises made for therapies for incurable diseases and conditions are staggering. Even the basic techniques of stem cell research are just now being tested, however, and the pace of gains in technique and the demise of broadly held theories have been startling.

A. Mechanisms

Pluripotent stem cells are those that are capable of forming any type of human tissue (e.g., blood, bone, neural tissue, etc.). In comparison, multipotent stem cells have lesser capacities to differentiate into other tissue. Once isolated, stem cells produce copies of themselves, creating a stem cell line that can renew itself indefinitely, although it is likely that the line eventually will decay or mutate. The techniques required to control cell death and prevent undesired differentiation are exacting.

Human embryonic stem cells (hESCs) are pluripotent stem cells that are withdrawn from a human

blastocyst, an early stage of embryonic development, occurring within 4–5 days of fertilization of
an ovum and having approximately 30 cells within
its inner cell mass. The most common technique for
withdrawing cells results in the destruction of the
blastocyst. A newer method may allow researchers
to withdraw one cell, potentially leaving the embryo
intact, with an entirely theoretical and probably
untestable possibility that the intact blastocyst
could be implanted in a woman's uterus and carried
to term.

More recently, researchers have created pluripotent stem cells from adult (i.e., from tissue harvested after birth) stem cell material. Adult pluripotent
stem cells may be found in umbilical cord blood, in
bone marrow, and in other tissue. Such naturally
pluripotent adult stem cells, however, are quite rare
and, thus, may be difficult to find and to harvest
from surrounding tissue. Newer techniques have
successfully developed pluripotent stem cells by ma-
nipulating adult cells that are more readily available.

Somatic cell nuclear transfer (SCNT) serves important functions in stem cell research. Stem cell
lines can be established, for example, by removing
the nucleus from a human ovum and inserting the
nucleus of another cell. The ovum then begins the
reproductive process, and when it reaches the blastocyst stage, a new stem cell line is established.
SCNT, known colloquially as cloning, is believed to
have the potential for creating tissue for transplantation that will overcome rejection by the recipient's

body as his own cell would have replaced the nucleus in the ovum.

B. Social and Ethical Issues

Social and ethical controversy over stem cell research has revolved around two related issues. The first issue relates to the moral status, if any, to be accorded to early human embryos. The second relates to the moral or social acceptability of cloning.

Some opponents of embryonic stem cell research argue that it is immoral to destroy or harm a human embryo, at least in the context of research if not in any context whatsoever. This argument follows the basic tenets of the pro-life or anti-abortion arguments discussed in Chapter 2. Some arguments supporting stem cell research hold that human embryos are indeed an early form of human life, but that the moral duty to relieve human suffering takes priority over any duty to preserve early embryos, especially at this very early embryonic stage and when those embryos are quite unlikely to be or will never be implanted for pregnancy and birth. Other proponents who do not agree that the blastocyst is a form of human life, argue that nevertheless it is a tissue that should be accorded some "special respect" due to its potential to form human life and that this respect is consistent with stem cell research. Finally, perhaps the currently dominant argument in support of stem cell research maintains that the blastocyst is in no way human life.

The mechanism of cloning (SCNT) is essentially the same no matter what its goal. Nevertheless, in the context of political debates and legislation on cloning, a distinction is made depending on the purpose for which the technique is employed. "Reproductive cloning" generally describes the potential use of SCNT to produce a complete human child. SCNT used in research is usually called "therapeutic cloning" in anticipation of future therapeutic interventions.

Reproductive cloning is broadly, although not universally, viewed as unacceptable based on concerns about its potential negative impact on children, families, and society. Therapeutic or research cloning is widely supported, although it is opposed by those who find manipulation and creation of human embryos immoral. See Section IV.C in Chapter 2.

C. Legal Issues

Some of the legal issues in stem cell research relate directly to the social and ethical controversies described in the previous section. For example, some state statutes ban reproductive cloning but allow or encourage therapeutic cloning; and other states have banned all forms of cloning or are silent on the matter.

Other legal issues relate to matters that are common in the context of research generally. These include, for example, patentability of the products and techniques of stem cell research and ownership of these products or techniques among researchers and among researchers and the contributors of the raw material. See Section V.B., above.

One issue that occurs in research generally but that has been raised with particularity in stem cell research is the acquisition of human tissue, in this case ova and embryos, for research. The first issue is whether the women who provide ova for stem cell research may be paid. Federal prohibitions against the sale of human tissue for transplantation ordinarily exempt payment for ova. See Section II.C in Chapter 7. Some states, however, have banned payments to women for ova to be used in stem cell research, although they permit payment for ova for in vitro fertilization services. Because women may be paid for ova used in in vitro fertilization, however, it may be possible to ask the seller and buyer in that transaction to permit excess ova not used in the IVF process to be used in research, provided no payment is made for that purpose or included within the original payment. The prohibition against payment is controversial, along the same lines as is payment for human organs for transplantation.

A second issue concerns whether researchers should be able to create new blastocysts using SCNT. One argument made in favor of human embryonic stem cell research is that the blastocysts used in that research would be confined to those left over from IVF treatments and that these embryos would otherwise be wasted by disposal or indefinite storage. Statutory restrictions and contract arrangements on the disposal of frozen embryos are at play here. See Section IV.B.2 in Chapter 2.

D. Federal Funding of Stem Cell Research

Federal law has never prohibited hESC research, although Congress has often considered proposed legislation that would do so, but there was no federal funding for such research. In 2001, then-President Bush issued an executive order allowing federal funding but only for research using human embryonic stem cell lines that existed prior to the date of the order. The rationale for this demarcation was that using stem cell lines that had already been established would not encourage the destruction of embryos, although it would put to use stem cell lines that had been produced through the earlier destruction of human embryos. President Obama's executive order in 2009, abandoned the cutoff date of the earlier order. The federal government is developing guidelines for hESC that would receive federal funds.

A federal statute (known as the Dickey–Wicker Amendment), however, continues to prohibit the use of federal funds for research that creates or discards, destroys, or subjects human embryos to risk of "injury or death." A prohibition against federal funding raises a significant although not insurmountable obstacle for academic research institutions as they must assure that the federal funds they receive for other research are not directly or remotely employed for stem cell research.

E.   State Regulation

As stem cell research progressed and while the federal government prohibited or restricted federal funding, many states enacted legislation to govern stem cell research within their borders. States have battled in their legislatures and in referenda over prohibiting stem cell research, usually in the form of banning any research that would create or destroy human embryos at any stage or by banning any form of human cloning. Several states ban payments for human ova or embryos for use in research, although this remains controversial. As discussed above, states vary in their laws concerning SCNT, with many banning reproductive cloning and some distinguishing between reproductive cloning, which may be prohibited, and therapeutic cloning, which may be permitted. See Section IV.C in Chapter 2. In contrast, several states have actively pursued hESC as a matter of economic development, making state funds available. Legislation and regulation authorizing state funding typically include provisions for some oversight of the research.

*

INDEX

References are to Pages

261

ARTIFICIAL INSEMINATION—Cont'd
Homologous (AI–H), 52
Procedure, 51, 55–56

ASSISTED REPRODUCTIVE TECHNOLOGIES (ART)
        See also Artificial Insemination; Cloning; In Vitro Fertilization; Surrogacy
    Generally, 49–55
And marriage, 75–76
Denial of services, 75–76

ASSISTING SUICIDE
See Physician Assisted Death

BABY DOE
See Children; Right to Die

BEST INTERESTS
        See also Children; Right to Die; Substituted Judgment
    Generally, 7–8, 132
Regarding fetus, 48
Regarding organ donation, 204
Regarding treatment for children, 154–155
Regarding parentage, 61–62, 73
Relation to substituted judgment, 133, 141

BIOBANKS
    Generally, 98–101
Federal regulations governing research, 224–225

BRAIN DEATH
See Determination of Death

CHILDREN
Abuse and neglect, 96, 155–156, 163, 165
As organ donors, 112–113, 195, 204
As research subjects, 234–238
Baby Doe, 161–164
Emancipated minors, 153
Health care decision making for, 152–172
Living wills, 135
Mature minor, 154
Newborn genetic screening, 94–98
Parens patriae, 96, 154
Reproductive decision making by, 36, 40, 47, 152

CLONING
        See also Stem Cell Research

†